JANE E. POLLOCK

Improving
Student
Learning

One
Teacher
at a Time

Association for Supervision and Curriculum Development ▪ Alexandria, Virginia USA

Association for Supervision and Curriculum Development
1703 N. Beauregard St. • Alexandria, VA 22311-1714 USA
Phone: 800-933-2723 or 703-578-9600 • Fax: 703-575-5400
Web site: www.ascd.org • E-mail: member@ascd.org
Author guidelines: www.ascd.org/write

Gene R. Carter, *Executive Director;* Nancy Modrak, *Director of Publishing;* Julie Houtz, *Director of Book Editing & Production;* Katie Martin, *Project Manager;* Georgia Park, *Senior Graphic Designer;* Valerie Younkin, *Desktop Publishing Specialist;* Dina Murray Seamon, *Production Specialist/Team Lead*

All Web links in this book are correct as of the publication date below but may have become inactive or otherwise modified since that time. If you notice a deactivated or changed link, please e-mail books@ascd.org with the words "Link Update" in the subject line. In your message, please specify the Web link, the book title, and the page number on which the link appears.

ASCD Member Book, No. FY07-6 (April 2007, PCR). ASCD Member Books mail to Premium (P), Comprehensive (C), and Regular (R) members on this schedule: Jan., PC; Feb., P; Apr., PCR; May, P; July, PC; Aug., P; Sept., PCR; Nov., PC; Dec., P.

PAPERBACK ISBN: 978-1-4166-0520-1   ASCD product #107005

Also available as an e-book through ebrary, netLibrary, and many online booksellers (see Books in Print for the ISBNs).

Quantity discounts for the paperback edition only: 10–49 copies, 10%; 50+ copies, 15%; for 1,000 or more copies, call 800-933-2723, ext. 5634, or 703-575-5634. For desk copies: member@ascd.org.

Library of Congress Cataloging-in-Publication Data

Pollock, Jane E., 1958-
  Improving student learning one teacher at a time / Jane E. Pollock.
    p. cm.
  Includes bibliographical references and index.
  ISBN 978-1-4166-0520-1 (pbk. : alk. paper) 1. Effective teaching—United States.
2. Academic achievement—United States. I. Title.
  LB1025.3.P65 2007
  371.102—dc22
                                                                    2006036883

18 17 16 15 14 13 12 11 10 09 08 07   1 2 3 4 5 6 7 8 9 10 11 12

For my parents,
Mary Ann and Bob Pollock

Improving Student Learning
One Teacher at a Time

Introduction

All, regardless of race or class or economic status, are entitled to a fair chance and to the tools for developing their individual powers of mind and spirit to the utmost. This promise means that all children by virtue of their own efforts, competently guided, can hope to attain the mature and informed judgment needed to secure gainful employment, and to manage their own lives, thereby serving not only their own interests but also the progress of society itself.

—A Nation at Risk

I FIRST MET SOCIAL STUDIES TEACHER GARY NUNNALLY IN THE FALL OF 2001 WHILE WE WERE attending a staff development seminar on instructional strategies in Lincoln, Nebraska. Sitting in front of me with his leg in a cast, Gary appeared to be giving me the dismissive "talk to the hand" signal with the underside of his foot. It was fitting, given the heated pedagogical exchange we were about to have. I clearly remember what started the volley: Gary good-naturedly bemoaned his students' disinterest in completing homework assignments and identified this lack of motivation as the cause of plummeting grades in his course, behavioral problems in his classroom, and, by extension, many uncomfortable parent-teacher encounters.

In response, I offered an audacious argument—at least, one that was audacious from Gary's point of view. Perhaps, I said, his homework assignments weren't worthy of his students' time. Maybe if he spent his energy improving the instruction in his classroom, the homework issue would sort itself out. In effect, I told Gary that he ought to focus less on what his students *weren't* doing at home and more on what he and they *were* doing in class.

So began our propitious relationship. Over the next three years, I persuaded Gary that if he wanted to see dramatic improvement in his students' achievement (or, as he put it, "in the grades"), he needed to make some changes in his planning, teaching, grading, and assessment practices. In turn, Gary convinced me that I'd need to change my own practices in staff development, curriculum development, and supervision.

Together, Gary and I came up with a simple but compelling pledge: "Everyone earns As and Bs in my classroom." This doesn't mean that Gary inflates students' grades or lowers his standards. It means that Gary is committed to planning provocative instruction and providing deliberate, systematic feedback sufficient to ensure that all his students will do A- and B-quality work and also perform at an advanced or proficient level on an external measure of achievement. In short, it means Gary is what makes the difference for his students. Without him as their teacher, they would *not* all do A and B work; they'd perform on the "normal curve," with some earning As and Bs, some earning Ds and Fs, and a good number in the middle earning Cs. It means Gary is the reason that his students understand what they need to learn and come to master the content. If he were not the teacher he is, his students would continue to see "doing better" in school as dependent on working harder and turning in homework on time.

The great news is that *any* willing teacher can do what Gary does. The process he follows is both the core of this book and the means to achieve its goal: improving student learning *one teacher at a time*.

We know what works in schools. In *Classroom Instruction That Works* (2001), Robert J. Marzano, Debra Pickering, and I cite various researchers who concur that "individual teachers can have a profound influence on student learning even in schools that are relatively ineffective" (p. 3). Knowing that teachers are the most important factor affecting learning is heartening for some educators but disheartening for others. "How do I know if I am an effective teacher?" they ask. "And if I find out that I'm *not* an effective teacher, what steps can I take to improve my pedagogy?" Simply put, you are an effective teacher if all your students learn—if they all meet the school's expectations or benchmarks at proficient or advanced levels for their grade level. And yes, teachers *can* improve their pedagogy. It's just a matter of reviewing and revising classroom practices, a process this book examines in depth.

Improving Student Learning One Teacher at a Time examines four principles that a teacher can employ in combination to improve student learning. These principles, which I call "the Big Four," are modifications of proven, fundamental practices that have evolved from the work of a variety of educators, including Madeline C. Hunter, Barak Rosenshine, Benjamin Bloom, Ralph Tyler, J. F. Herbart, John Goodlad, Grant Wiggins, Bruce Joyce, Beverly Showers, and Robert J. Marzano. Each of these researchers and theorists has addressed specific issues, ranging from teacher planning to student assessment. Each of them has contributed enormously to the field, and over the years, each new publication of theirs has seemed to be the apogee of school improvement solutions. My epiphany was that merging significant ideas conveyed in these works into a single, concise heuristic—one that any teacher can replicate—is what's needed to truly transform student learning and move the "normal" distribution of student performance to all *A*s and *B*s. Most important, adhering to the Big Four doesn't require dramatic, districtwide initiatives; when individual teachers make these key adjustments to familiar practices, student learning improves significantly.

We begin with Chapter 1's detailed introduction to the Big Four and a respectful acknowledgment that past practices in improving student learning in the United States have been based in hope rather than certainty: "I *hope* this lesson works." "I *hope* the students will do the homework." "I *hope* the class will do well on the test." The time has come for teachers to expect success rather than hope for it. The Big Four approach offers a way to do this through the use of (1) precise terminology to describe what students will learn; (2) purposeful instructional planning and delivery; (3) purposeful assessment; and (4) the application of deliberate assessment and feedback strategies to improve learning for all students in the classroom. I believe that with today's technology and resources at our disposal, through this process we *can* take hope out of schools and replace it with confident action.

Chapter 2 begins the focused examination of each of the Big Four with an explanation of how to design a classroom curriculum document that's truly useful, and thus, unlikely to join the collection of curriculum documents now gathering dust on your shelf. Because today's educators can access curriculum documents online, on district networks, and from international and national reports, they can align their curriculum with state, national, and international frameworks while still ensuring its relevance to daily classroom activities. The curriculum documents, focused on clearly articulated learning targets, can be easily shared and disseminated: cut and pasted, revised, e-mailed, and Googled. And both research and common sense tell us that a teacher who uses clearly articulated learning targets is more likely to help students reach those targets than a teacher who buries these targets in a dusty binder.

Chapter 3 examines how to plan instruction in a manner that maximizes student learning. It introduces the Teaching Schema for Master Learners (TSML), a new approach to lesson planning that I have adapted from the model articulated in Madeline C. Hunter's *Mastery Teaching* (1982), Barak Rosenshine's six teaching steps in direct instruction (1997), and the works of 19th-century philosopher, psychologist, and educator J. F. Herbart (see Gutek, 1991). The key concept is this: When teachers regularly plan using a schema based on how learners learn, such planning becomes second nature. A teacher who operates with this "pedagogical automaticity"—who proceeds deliberately and without worrying, "What am I going to do next?"—will have more class time to address student needs and provide better feedback.

Chapter 4 discusses assessment. Once a teacher has identified the appropriate learning targets, any number of assessment strategies can provide evidence of satisfactory student performance or, conversely, the need for further instruction. Although most teachers agree on the benefits of assessments that require students to think rather than simply recall information or procedures, here in the United States, recent shifts in education policy have pushed the pendulum back toward standardized testing. The unfortunate result is that many teachers have abandoned the power of robust, self-designed classroom assessments. Planning effective assessment of student learning that incorporates varied question types, opportunities for self-assessment, and even simple observation ought to go hand in hand with instructional planning focused on stated learning targets. This chapter shows you how to do that.

Chapter 5 addresses the keystone of the Big Four: feedback. Virtually ignored as an influence on learning by previous teaching theories, feedback is essential to improving student achievement and pedagogical practices. But when most teachers reflect on their feedback practices—verbal, written, and in the form of record keeping or reporting—they realize that the feedback they provide is often aimed at modifying student behavior or ensuring task completion rather than facilitating learning. What's more, the feedback they provide is generally not very timely, further limiting its usefulness. By contrast, adhering to the Big Four approach means teachers provide students with meaningful feedback aligned with benchmarks in a timely manner, ensuring that the feedback actually affects learning. Chapter 5 also addresses the efficacy of feedback at the administrative level. If feedback works well for students, it can also work for teachers. When a principal uses the same schema applied to instructional planning to provide meaningful feedback to instructors, teaching improves and the entire organization transforms, one teacher at a time.

In addition to exploring a primary theme, each chapter in this book considers the availability of computer software and information-sharing advances, both of which allow teachers to easily cross geographical boundaries in the quest to improve pedagogy and student learning. Sharing videotapes or DVDs that document classroom activity, creating blogs, contributing to electronic posting boards, e-mailing, and participating in video conferencing can all improve performance at little added cost to the teacher or school.

Finally, throughout this book, I've included the perspectives of educators who have embraced the Big Four approach. Using their own words, these teachers share their experiences and those of their colleagues, relating tales of enthusiasm, reluctance, and change. Each pays tribute to the reward of patiently and steadfastly transforming his or her personal pedagogy, a colleague's perspective and practice, or student performances . . . one teacher at a time.

1

Replacing Hope with Certainty

The Big Four approach provides a way for each individual teacher
to improve the learning of every student. Adhering to the Big Four
means

- Using precise terminology to describe what students will learn
- Undertaking purposeful instructional planning and delivery
- Employing purposeful assessment
- Applying deliberate assessment and feedback strategies

"TAKE HOPE OUT OF SCHOOLS" SEEMS AN INCONGRUOUS SLOGAN TO EMPLOY IN THE QUEST
to improve learning, but if you recall any number of comments you and your
colleagues are likely to have made, its relevance becomes clear: "I *hope* this lab
works; I spent a lot of time collecting the specimens and setting it up for my
students." "I *hope* the students can identify the adverbs and adjectives on the
test; we spent so much time reviewing." "I *hope* that tonight's concert goes well,
I am so nervous, even though every section has worked hard and we went over
every piece again in today's rehearsal." "I *hope* they learned it; I guess next year's
teacher will find out."

How did we get to the point where teachers *hope* for good results rather
than *plan* for them?

Teachers throughout the United States and in other countries are determined to do what it takes to improve learning, improve teaching, and improve

schooling, but their efforts are frequently frustrated from the start. Typically, teachers attend staff development sessions to learn a new technique or tactic. But no matter how successful the initial session, when the training ends and these teachers return to the classroom, hope once again takes over: "I *hope* I get to try this new technique, and I *hope* it brings improved results!" Educator and researcher Bruce Joyce reminds us that learning disconnected topics in staff development programs without systematic follow-up does not positively affect student learning (Sparks, 1998).

To take hope out of school and replace it with certainty, teachers need more robust pedagogical tools that we can use to improve student leaning in every subject area and in any classroom. The Big Four approach is one such tool.

The Big Four

The tenets of the Big Four are as follows:

1. *Use a well-articulated curriculum.* Know and use clearly articulated learning targets—ones that are robust concepts, generalizations, or procedures rather than only statements of daily classroom objectives.

2. *Plan for delivery.* Plan and use instructional strategies that will help the learner remember content and apply information and skills rather than just do schoolwork.

3. *Vary assessment.* Use a range of assessment methods to clarify the learner's status relative to learning targets, and generate the information necessary to help the learner achieve these targets.

4. *Give criterion-based feedback.* Give methodical feedback to the learner based on the targets, and refine record keeping and reporting accordingly.

Many teachers are likely to say that they are already implementing the Big Four. Certainly they have a curriculum, create lesson plans, use some authentic assessment techniques, and give feedback in the form of grades. But if we ask these same teachers if all their students perform to their expectations, we might get a very different set of reactions—possibly including some that shift the blame for failure to the students: "I did my best, but the students didn't do their part." Such thinking traps us in the cycle of teaching for ourselves; that is, teaching to become "master teachers" rather than teaching to create a classroom of "master learners." It's a subtle difference but an important one. Focusing on our improvement as instructors does not necessarily lead to our students' improvement as learners.

Historically, the dominant public education trends in the United States have encouraged this "master teacher" approach. Understanding the evolution of our current pedagogy provides a starting point for shifting our focus toward teaching and scoring to standards or grade-level benchmarks, thus ensuring that we don't have to simply *hope* that our students learn.

Not a New Idea

In 1956, Benjamin Bloom wrote that as educators, we should create a taxonomy of educational objectives to promote the exchange of best ideas and materials and use these objectives in testing to improve student achievement. Guided by "Bloom's taxonomy," educators have spent the last 50 years trying different curriculum designs to get "just-right" targets that will improve student knowledge and information application. Knowing and using robust, well-articulated learning targets is the first step in the implementation of the Big Four.

We can compare the evolution of curriculum and learning targets to the evolution of human flight. Numerous failed efforts preceded the famous Kitty Hawk launch, but each of those failures provided vital information that led to the Wright brothers' eventual success. Similarly, the Big Four learning targets were informed by earlier, unsuccessful designs. What characteristics of these previous designs looked good at the time but proved ineffectual over the long term? And how are we changing benchmarks so that they are more than the same old "objectives" or "outcomes" called by a new name?

Curriculum and Purpose

In *Basic Principles of Curriculum and Instruction* (1949), Ralph Tyler raised four questions he deemed most significant to curriculum development:

1. What educational purposes should the school seek to attain?
2. What educational experiences can the school provide to attain these purposes?

3. How can these educational experiences be effectively organized?

4. How can we determine if these purposes are being attained?

The answer to Tyler's first question depends on what point you're looking at on the timeline of education's evolution. Prior to the 19th century, the perceived purpose of education was either religious, meant to inculcate children with the theology of those doing the teaching, or pragmatic, meant to ensure an economically and socially useful populace. In what was to become the United States, most educational bodies followed the European model of social class separation. Children were either educated or they were not, and those who *were* received the kind of education commensurate with their role in society: classical learning for members of the gentry, apprenticeships for tradesmen, and so on.

The debate surrounding learning targets began in earnest during the Industrial Revolution, when the need for technical education to prepare workers for specialized occupations came up against the "general knowledge" approach thought to provide the foundation for social efficiency. This debate gave birth to the development of the "modern" school. At this point in history, the curriculum question was clear: Do we design curricula or learning targets that are primarily vocational in nature or primarily academic?

Tyler credits the early 1900s' Committee of Ten (which established a curricular alternative to classical teachings) and later, the Commission on the Reorganization of Secondary Education (which offered a more liberal arts approach to education) for struggling to address the question of education's purpose in the United States. As the first half of the 20th century came to a close, there was a general consensus that education's purpose was twofold: to create cultural literacy and patriotism and, more importantly, to catapult the U.S. economy into its place as a world leader in trade. In addition, most states' obligatory education laws at last offered the opportunity for learning to all children regardless of socioeconomic status, thus moving the nation closer to Thomas Jefferson's vision of one in which all citizens are educated so that they might vote wisely. "I know of no safe depository of the ultimate powers of the society but the people themselves," Jefferson wrote in 1820. "[I]f we think them not enlightened enough to exercise their control with wholesome discretion, the remedy is not to take it from them, but to inform their discretion by education."

Objectives for Educational Experiences

The post–World War II baby boom led to significant growth in the school-age population and a shift in educational focus toward answering Tyler's second and third questions, concerning educational experiences and their organization. The call came for new kinds of curriculum and new ways to design learning targets.

The first of these ways was Bloom's taxonomy. The actual document, *Taxonomy of Educational Objectives* (1956), was developed by a committee of 34 college and university examiners and edited by Benjamin Bloom. He and his colleagues argued that a classification system for educational objectives would enable teachers to plan instruction and assessment tasks relative to stated goals and then discuss learning progress in a technical and logical way. They recommended a classification of learning in cognitive, affective, and psychomotor areas, suggesting that the clarity it would bring would parallel the increased accuracy of understanding biologists achieved by organizing the complex details of the natural world into categories like kingdom, phylum, class, order, and so on. When applied to schools, the taxonomy would allow teachers to discuss student learning based on a clear set of targets, which would facilitate student success. The authors clarified their goals thusly: "We are not attempting to classify the instructional methods used by the teachers, the ways in which teachers relate themselves to students or the different kinds of instructional materials they use. We are not attempting to classify the particular subject matter or content. What we are classifying is the intended behavior of students—the ways in which individuals are to act, think, or feel as a result of participating in some unit of instruction" (Bloom, 1956, p. 12).

The learning targets advocated by Bloom and his colleagues, then, were a general structure and not precise knowledge or skills; they did not give the teacher explicit guidance to teach to, and track, student performance. (We would have to wait 40 more years, until the 1990s, for the development of comprehensive "particular subject matter or content.") Whatever the taxonomy's initial limitations, it provided a durable structure for communicating about thinking and learning. Its emphasis on knowledge, comprehension, application, analysis, synthesis, and evaluation established the standard for contemporary instructional programs and assessment tasks (see the second and third tenets of the Big Four). It also introduced the idea of targets (i.e., information and skills) that students can learn to perform at the higher levels of analysis, synthesis, and evaluation, rather than just remembering information for a recall or comprehension test.

Two other methods for designing learning targets also populated the pedagogical landscape in the second half of the 20th century: Robert Mager's three-part approach and Gronlund's general-to-specific approach. Mager (1962) produced behavioral objectives that sought to address the performance measurement dilemma. His design took into account cognitive or psychomotor behavior, the condition imposed on the learner, and the proficiency level acceptable for that behavior. Anyone familiar with writing behavioral objectives in curriculum guides probably remembers the lengthy and complicated process required to manage all three of Mager's components in one statement of performance without feeling overwhelmed by the breadth of content or bothered by the disconnect between the depth of subject knowledge and alleged proficiency. Gronlund (1978) suggested that the breadth of content knowledge lent itself to organizing principles that moved from one general objective to multiple, specific objectives. His approach did not specifically address achievement measurement; it offered instead a flexible schema or scaffold of questions one could ask to create a particular set of objectives, leaving the breadth of the curriculum development work to the teacher or school to complete.

So began today's method of curriculum development. Discouraged by the lack of time set aside for curriculum development, the breadth of the content knowledge thought necessary to meet the demands of cultural literacy, and uncertainty about "writing curriculum" (Which development method is best? The taxonomy? Mager's methodology? Gronlund's?), many teachers complied with the curriculum-writing task by simply using the textbook as their classroom curriculum. They learned to make their own decisions about what to teach and what to leave out, guided chiefly by the amount of content in the textbook and the length of the school year. At times, of course, that approach left subject-area gaps or created topic-area overlaps for the students.

Teachers hoped that by teaching to the textbook as curriculum, their students would "move up" on Bloom's taxonomy. Conquering the textbook became the goal, and its contents the de facto curriculum; teachers used activities geared toward apprehending the textbook content, gave tests on that content, and assigned grades based on the test results. You see within these developments the skeleton of the Big Four taking shape. However, what we hadn't yet figured out was that learning targets could, and should, be better than textbook activities.

Reexamining the Purpose of Education

Thirty years after the landmark classification of educational goals, a new sense of urgency forced educators into redesigning learning targets. *A Nation at Risk*, published in 1983 by the U.S. Department of Education, held schools responsible for the nation's predicted slide from the zenith of the world's economy, noting that "while we can take justifiable pride in what our schools and colleges have historically accomplished and contributed to the United States and the well-being of its people, the educational foundations of our society are presently being eroded by a rising tide of mediocrity that threatens our very future as a nation and a people" (p. 1). A second report, *What Work Requires of Schools, SCANS—Report on Workplace Skills* (U.S. Department of Labor, 1991), issued a warning to parents: "Parents must insist that their sons and daughters master this [workplace] know-how and that their local schools teach it. Unless you do, your children are unlikely to earn a decent living" (p. 5).

These two reports sent teachers across the nation back to curriculum committees trying feverishly to couple the former's "new basics" with the latter's "workplace know-how." The result was a briefly used yet highly memorable type of learning target design: outcome-based education.

Australian aboriginal culture tells of a mythical creature call the bunyip, which possesses every physical characteristic of every type of the continent's extraordinary animal life. If ever a decade produced a curricular bunyip, it was the outcome-driven 1980s. An *outcome* was defined as bigger than an objective but smaller than a K–12 goal. It included subject content but was not limited to schoolwork tasks, meaning it also described appropriate preparation for the workplace. In other words, outcome statements had tails, scales, flippers, a pouch, and every other imaginable characteristic. They remained as elusive as the legendary monster of the outback and could never be measured.

The eventual demise of the outcome led, in the 1990s, to the promising rise of content-specific standards and benchmarks. Driven by the need to create the cantilevered specificity in the content areas alluded to in Bloom's cognitive taxonomy, various private and public educational organizations published more than 100 standards documents, mobilizing to strengthen academic achievement in math, science, social studies, language arts, the fine and practical arts, and technology. Using and testing those targets became the focus of the No Child Left Behind era.

The New Idea

So, it seems that we have been working on learning targets for a very long time: from Thomas Jefferson's *Bill for the More General Diffusion of Knowledge,* introduced in 1779, to President George W. Bush's No Child Left Behind, signed in 2002. Skimming history, we notice that U.S. educators slowly ceased to debate Tyler's purpose of schooling. Even as they continued to quibble over the format of curriculum documents, they agreed on the underlying rationale for having a curriculum: to improve teaching, to help teachers communicate among themselves, and to give teachers a clear instructional path to follow or modify for their own purposes, according to their own preferences.

The message of the 1990s standards movement was direct: What was needed were robust cultural literacy statements, called *standards and benchmarks,* to describe precisely what students should know and be able to do. They were to be written in a spiraled manner, reminiscent of J. F. Herbart's or Hilda Taba's suggestions; articulated across the grade levels; and measurable through both classroom tasks and some form of external measure, such as a standardized test.

The advent of standards and benchmarks brought a subtle but crucial change to how educators approached curriculum development—a change fundamental to the Big Four approach. We now create learning targets in our curriculum documents for the express purpose of improving student learning; these targets may only incidentally improve a teacher's craft or communication. Teachers who use a "just-right set of benchmarks" can track student progress and performance to those benchmarks and adjust instruction accordingly to help students attain mastery. The benchmarks themselves—robust concepts, generalizations, and procedures—when used to plan for instruction and assessment, and coupled with explicit feedback, are hardy enough to improve student learning. That is the essence of the Big Four.

Are We There Yet?

Let's review Tyler's questions about curriculum development and the generally accepted answers at our particular point in education's timeline:

1. *What educational purposes should the school seek to attain?* Education's purpose is to ensure that all children between the approximate ages of 6 and 16 have the opportunity to receive publicly funded schooling, resulting in the possibility of upward social mobility and the ability of all citizens to uphold the tenets of a free and democratic society.

2. *What educational experiences can schools provide to attain these purposes?* The classroom experiences will be designed by teachers who are trained to teach by the university research and evaluation system.

3. *How can schools most effectively organize these experiences?* The teachers will organize activities and assessments based on modern psychological and neurological theories.

4. *How can schools determine whether these purposes are being attained?* Schools will meet effective school criteria, such as providing a safe and orderly environment, developing and adhering to a clear school mission, ensuring time-on-task, and having high expectations for student achievement.

Note that each of Tyler's questions focuses on the school as an organization. Over the years, they've led us to the same research on effective schools and the same answers first offered by James S. Coleman (1966) and verified over and over since: Absent really strong intervention, each school is only as good as the socioeconomic status of the neighborhood in which it is located. Knowing this, we've tried to improve schools' effectiveness through various iterations of school effectiveness units or school improvement plans. Although we have made some progress throughout the years, educators today face a new challenge. Quite simply, students in today's classrooms are different from their predecessors.

Students Are Different Today

I remember being surprised when I read the statistics laid out in John Good-lad's *A Place Called School* (1984): "In 1950, only half of the white and a quarter of the black school-age population graduated from high school" (p. 12). These numbers seem paltry for a nation that started with a vision of a fully educated population and had been ostensibly working toward that vision for 170 years.

Arguably, a goal of education improvement is to identify which students or groups of students do not attend or complete school and figure out how to change that pattern. Historical records can be enlightening, but as we learn from Tom Snyder's *120 Years of American Education: A Statistical Portrait* (1993), attempts to examine these statistics and use them as the basis for generalizations and improvement ideas are complicated by overlapping data and shifting definitions of what it meant to "complete" education. What we can say with certainty is that although overall public school enrollment and attendance rose significantly throughout the 20th century, rates of actual completion or graduation increased far less dramatically. In addition, those students who were enrolled, actually attended, and went on to graduate were a fairly homogeneous lot. Generally speaking, this group excluded large numbers of children living in poverty; children who labored on family farms or in family businesses; children who were physically or cognitively disabled; children who were nonwhite or recent immigrants; and children we might think of as "Huck Finns"—those who opted to drop out rather than submit to the drill of academics. Additionally, those students who stayed in school until graduation were those who did well in school; those who didn't do well left without too many questions asked.

Today's classrooms are a different place. We celebrate diversity and open the doors of public schools to all children, regardless of race, origin, ability, socioeconomic status, or gender. Appropriately, the focus of our curriculum has expanded to suit this more varied student population, and our school improvement efforts are driven by a commitment to help all the students in our classrooms learn and make progress.

Are Teachers Different Today?

Recently, in a professional development seminar, I asked a novice teacher how she had learned to teach. Her immediate answer: "I learned from my teachers."

Teasingly, I responded, "Certainly you mean you learned from your college professors?"

"No," she replied confidently, "I mean from my school teachers."

If you agree with this teacher, and with a premise put forth by Jim Stigler, coauthor (with James Hiebert) of *The Teaching Gap* (1999) and (with Harold Stevenson) *The Learning Gap* (1992), you believe that we learned to teach from our own elementary and secondary teachers. When we were sitting in classroom as students, day after day, year after year, we were building and solidifying neural networks that defined for us what teaching was. These patterns of thought made it difficult for us to significantly change our pedagogical behaviors once we started teaching. So, if we learned to teach from our teachers, and they learned to teach from their teachers, and so on, one could argue that many of us today have teaching habits that stretch back to the 1950s—instructional, assessment, grading, and record-keeping strategies inherited from teachers who were responsible for instructing only half of today's students, both in terms of numbers and demographics. I'm reminded of a conversation I had with veteran educator who talked about her experience in the Denver Public School system more than 60 years ago. She taught classes that averaged about 42 students—not one of them a "motivation" or "behavioral" problem. "It was not hard to teach well in those days," she avowed.

To succeed with the students who are in our classrooms now, we need to incorporate different learning tools, such as the ones described in the second and third tenets of the Big Four. However, we should not forget that the teaching tools used in the 1950s *did work for many students.* As we explore the principles of the Big Four, you'll see that they do not throw out the baby with the bathwater.

The *New* Effective Teacher Movement for the 21st Century

My teaching colleagues and I know we would have been great teachers in the 1950s. But it is not the 1950s. It is time, then, for us to make some deliberate changes in our definition of an effective school. In order for Goodlad's "Place Called School" to be worthy—a place where all children between the ages of 6 and 16 have the opportunity to succeed in publicly funded education—we need to update our current practices commensurate with the changes in school populations, technology, and neuropsychology.

Here, then, is a summary of our country's curricular history. In 1956, Bloom suggested that having curricula would improve learning (we might think of this as "the Big One"). Two decades later, Madeline Hunter added that for teachers to use curricula effectively, they must become master teachers ("the Big Two"). Grant Wiggins's addendum came 10 years after that: a recommendation of authentic assessment ("the Big Three"). Teachers were improving their craft in the late 1980s, but they still sanctioned the normal curve of student learning. Looking back, the Big Three left out one very critical player: *the student.* The targets were simply the teaching targets. With the Big Four, the targets are robust statements designed to generate feedback to the individual learner. Giving this direct, benchmark-specific feedback is essential to moving all students toward higher levels of learning and achievement.

Remember: The most important factor affecting individual student success in schools is the classroom teacher (Marzano, Pickering, & Pollock, 2001). You can have a significant effect on your group of students; you can do what Gary Nunnally does and "push the normal curve for all learners" when you (1) use a well-articulated curriculum, (2) plan for delivery, (3) vary assessment, and (4) give criterion-based feedback. What's more, you know how to do this because you inherited the "genetic code" for the Big Four from your own teachers. Now it's just a matter of honing curriculum targets, planning instruction to those targets, and preparing a useful feedback mechanism in your delivery, assessment, and grading.

Teacher Voice

Gary Nunnally

"As is the teacher, so is the school." These are the words of Victor Cousin, secretary to the board of the first normal school in the United States. They are just as true today as when Cousin wrote them back in 1839. In the following section, Gary, a secondary social studies teacher, tells about his journey from being what he considered to be a good teacher to becoming a great one. It is a reminder of why we must examine and revise our practices, an acknowledgment of what these kinds of revisions entail, and an ode to perseverance. Changes in the Big Four don't happen overnight. But, as Gary found, they will happen if you are committed to the outcomes they promise: gains for students, for the teacher, and for the school.

....

AFTER NEARLY 10 YEARS OF TEACHING MIDDLE AND HIGH SCHOOL STUDENTS, PROFESSIONAL development sessions had come to seem like just one more thing to do. I had to be dragged kicking and screaming to "one more PD class" on September 11, 2001. I planned to grade papers.

Other than the world-altering events of that day, what made this session different from all the others I had attended was the career-changing effect the training would eventually have on my classroom. It began with Janie Pollock posing this seemingly harmless, but nonetheless illuminating question: "Is your classroom good enough for my sons, Sam and Zachary?" I was completely taken aback.

At that time I had two children, Joshua and Elizabeth, and I have come to refer to the process I began that day as the "Josh and Ellie test." Would this lesson plan be good enough if Josh and Ellie were sitting in my classroom? I had to acknowledge that although I worked hard and wanted to be as effective a teacher as possible, I was falling short. More specifically, my classroom was not focused on learning; it was focused on grades and points. As difficult as it is to admit, I came to the realization that my own classroom was not passing the "Josh and Ellie test."

A Recovering Gradeaholic

I write today as a recovering *gradeaholic*. Ralph Waldo Emerson said that "Rings and other jewels are not gifts, but apologies. The only gift is a portion of thyself." Giving "a portion of thyself" can mean many things for a teacher. One thing it definitely means is *time*.

I do not have more time than any other teacher. But now I don't spend the majority of my time grading every assignment, assigning arbitrary numbers or points for completion, and taking off another arbitrary percentage of points for things like tardiness. Now I spend that time with my students, focused on their learning and enjoying teaching as a planning, delivery, and assessment process. Sometimes, it is a reteaching process.

Early in the transformation of my classroom, I asked my students what happens between kindergarten and 8th, 9th, or 11th grade. As a guy in his 30s who loves learning, it has always bothered me when kids in my classroom do not share this passion. When I drop my kindergartner off at school, he is so excited to go and learn. Why does that attitude change? My students gave the typical responses about how school is boring, predictable, and really about making the grade with individual teachers, not about learning the content. If the teacher likes you, they said, you get a better grade, but you could also get good grades by doing extra projects. The students surprised me with the comment that we teachers are addicted to giving grades. I certainly was.

My Big Four Transformation

I am a work in progress. I'm reminded of Coach John Wooden's words: "It's what you learn after you know it all that really counts" and "Once you are finished learning, you are finished." My comments about my four-year transformation do not indicate a state of "arrival." I am still transforming. In fact, I am energized by the changes that continue to take place in my classroom. However, it's helpful to examine the first four years of my transformation, where it is easier to trace the specific changes to my pedagogical automaticity.

Year One: Listening and Learning. I'm embarrassed to admit it, but before my transformation, I was already tired by October. I was tired of the same conversations producing the same results—tired of the same kids failing, the same kids being disengaged from learning, and the same kids causing the same classroom management problems. None of these problems was fully remedied in my first year of using the Big Four approach, but the process of transforming my classroom had begun. I was dutifully attending the training sessions with Janie Pollock, taking notes, and asking a lot of questions. In addition, I was beginning to rewrite, not just edit, my lesson plans using a new lesson schema: the Teaching Schema for Master Learners.

Toward the end of year number one, I stopped giving points for homework. Like it would be for any other addict, this first step was a difficult one for me. I did not really understand the whole process and I gave up this practice reluctantly. To be certain, I was not yet ready to stop giving points for quizzes and projects! At this juncture, I naively thought the problem in my classroom was the points. And I was fixing that.

Year Two: From Points to Performance. During the second year, I began planning with another 7th grade history teacher. Yes, I finally cracked open the proverbial "closed door." (You know the one: "This is my classroom, this is how I've always taught, and this is how I'm going to continue teaching.") Once a week, this colleague and I got together during our planning time and mapped out where we were headed with our students that week. While we coplanned all year together, I also began testing and grading to the district-provided standards to which we were both teaching. My coplanner thought I was crazy to use only tests (not homework, participation, and behavior) to determine students' grades, but because he saw the benefit of planning together, we at least continued to meet.

In the meantime, I assigned my first project without any "points," just grading to the standards and benchmarks. I created a rubric to assess students and guide their work: to help them know what an incomplete, emerging, proficient, and exemplary project looks like. There would be no points assigned as "grade boosters" (e.g., points for presentation, timeliness, and so on).

Before I gave my students the assignment, I called my friend Gerry Larson at district staff development for moral support. I said, "Let me make sure that I've got this straight." (Remember, I am a recovering gradeaholic!) "I am going to give more than 140 middle school students a project that will take about one week to complete, and I am not going to make it worth any points. What will motivate them if they cannot earn points?" Gerry calmly reminded me that I was scoring to the benchmarks, not gathering points. As I hung up the phone, I felt a combination of emotions—fear, as well as a tinge of "Hey, something exciting is happening here." As I look back on it, it was a very freeing feeling. I was beginning to emerge from my self-imposed reliance on points—beginning to let the benchmarks guide not just my teaching but also students' learning.

As I delivered the project instructions to my students, I broke out in a sweat. I had visions of my principal walking through the door and seeing my students completely off-task, standing on desks, singing, dancing, and totally out of control. I just knew I was going to get fired. And then, the epiphany: I had not been using the assessment process to improve student achievement; I had been using points to *control student behavior*.

And, wouldn't you know it, my students appeared motivated to complete the assignment the same way they would have under the old points system. That is, some students produced exemplary projects, many completed the assignment satisfactorily, and a number of students performed unacceptably. Although I'd taken a critical step toward implementing the Big Four, I was still teaching in much the same way I had before, except without the security blanket of "points." I would need to make more changes before the level of my students' learning truly transformed.

I took the elimination of points a step further and began giving students quizzes that were not worth any points. Of course my students would invariably ask, "Mr. Nunnally, how much is number two worth? How many points should I take off for missing number three?" I would calmly reply that I did not want them to take any points off; I wanted them to understand what they had missed so they could make the necessary improvements. I would urge them to fill in the answer correctly, making sure they knew why they had missed it. This new way of grading was a continuous learning process for my kids. It took some students longer to get it than others. Sometimes, in exasperation, I would tell students, "Fine, today's quiz is worth 5,000 points" or "Take 100 points off if you miss number four!" Usually this helped to clarify the goal; it was about learning social studies, not about accumulating more points in social studies.

Just because I was not giving points for daily work, projects, and quizzes doesn't mean that my students were not receiving feedback, nor does it mean that there were no points assigned for test performance. As I tell my students, "Friday night, the lights will be on, the cheerleaders will be there, and we'll be keeping score. In the meantime, continue to work hard at your preparation so you'll be ready for your performance on the test." Then, when the students get ready to take their exam, I no longer say, "Good luck." Instead, I say, "I hope that you perform as well as you have prepared." I found that what Janie had said during that first professional development session was true: "It's all about feedback; it's all about giving feedback to 'just-right' characteristics to make improvements."

A new addition to my pedagogy emerged: I asked to team with our media specialist. After a typical exam, I would spend the next day with the students who were not proficient in achieving the learning objectives. Our media specialist would provide enrichment activities and lessons for the students who had already performed at a proficient level on their learning objectives. For instance, at the time, I taught 7th grade world history. Our first unit was a geography unit. The students who performed at a proficient level got to make a "trading card" of a country, similar to baseball or football trading cards, complete with fascinating facts about that country. I laminated the cards for them. I knew I was on to something when the students who had to retest (and, thus, had missed out on the enrichment activity) asked if they could make a card on their own and have me laminate it for them. Now, this was a process that was passing the "Josh and Ellie test"!

Year Three: The Dip. During the third year of transformation, I accepted a new job in a different district, purely for family reasons. I was excited about the new job and about the district. But before too long, my excitement was drained by the teaching approach favored by my new school.

Remember the Burger King commercial featuring an elderly lady yelling, "Where's the beef?" As I began preparing my lesson plans, I wanted to yell, "Where are the benchmarks?" For two years, I had worked hard to reassess my teaching and create lesson plans that began with clearly stated benchmarks and objectives. Now I had moved to a new district that expected me to teach thematically without a clear set of benchmarks.

This expectation posed a new challenge. I worked hard to implement the expectations of my district while at the same time putting together a set of benchmarks on my own.

Year Four: The Lights Are On and the Cheerleaders Are There. The fourth year of my transformation brought an amazing, and utterly unexpected, revelation: My principal came into the classroom to observe me, and I realized I was teaching the lesson the same way I would on any other day. For years I had fretted over my lesson when I knew my principal would be observing me. How could I make the lesson *really* exciting? How could I make sure my students were *really* engaged in their learning that day? Maybe they would have mercy on me, notice the principal was there, and at least *act* like they were interested. Instead, during this fourth year, I made lesson plans using the TSML schema, as I do every other day of the year, and taught the lesson without worrying about the presence of my principal; I had achieved a new pedagogical automaticity. There was nothing out of the ordinary about the lesson that day—just rich conversations with my students as we discussed and engaged in the learning process. What a feeling!

The Resistance

When I changed districts during that third year of my transformation, part of my new job was to coach the school's basketball team, with the clear expectation on my part (and the administration's) that I was coming to build the program into championship form. At the beginning of our first year together, the team and I established our theme for the basketball program: "New Season . . . New Dreams." During that first year, people would frequently tell me, "You can't do this; you can't do that; we've never done it that way before." I would then explain that one definition of insanity is to do things the way they've always been done and expect different results. In other words, if they expected different results from the basketball team, as I did, then we really did need to make this a new season with new dreams and work hard to achieve them. The resistance to "the transformation" in my classroom had been no less intense.

I remember realizing that when I started truly adhering to the Big Four principles, my classroom experience became much more intense. It reminded me of the intensity of a well-planned and executed basketball practice. As the teacher, I really was ultimately responsible for how my students did. No longer would grades be "padded" by daily work and extra credit. My students' grades would simply be a reflection of their learning. If my students were failing, they were not learning; and if they were not learning, it was my job to help them improve their learning! No longer could I think or say, "Well, if the student would just turn in his homework . . ."

Meet the Parents

Back in year two, members of my 7th grade team asked me to come to a meeting to compile a list of our students who were failing. We would mail a letter home to parents advising them that their child was failing. Then they would receive a mid-quarter report that invariably showed their child was still failing. We followed up in both cases to make sure the parents had received the notices, ensuring that they and the students were advised before receiving the final quarter grade.

Now, what educator or parent can deny the importance of maintaining open communication with parents? It is certainly important that parents are properly apprised of their child's standing in class. My point is not to knock my team members' efforts at communication. But these were conversations about points, and lack of points, rather than conversations about student learning.

When I informed my team members that, in fact, I did not have any failing students (for the first time in 10 years of teaching middle and high school students), I was met with a combination of disbelief and scorn. ("Nunnally must really be lowering his standards!") My alienation was only compounded when the team replied, "That's OK, just come and write letters to the parents of the kids who have zeroes for not turning in assignments," and I had to tell them that I didn't have any students with zeroes. (These days, my students process all of their assignments in an individual notebook, which is a work in progress. They can always go back and add to their notes and improve their learning.) When I look back on these experiences, I realize that although they were motivated by good intentions, all of the meetings and notifications were just smoke and mirrors—a replacement for real learning and progress.

Given my experiences, I can appreciate the importance of implementing change in a team environment with administrative support. At the time, I was alone among my colleagues, trying to make massive changes to my pedagogy with only the support of Gerry Larson and Janie Pollock. How empowering it is to be at a school where my principal is an instructional leader, encouraging positive changes that are based on sound principles.

Many people have asked me about the response my students' parents have had to my Big Four transformation. In the past, I was always nervous about parent-teacher conferences. How would the parents respond to their child failing? What would they think of the zeroes their child had received and the resultant effect on her overall grade? Well, by the end of the second year of the transformation, I was looking forward to parent-teacher conferences. Just as I did in the classroom, I made the focus of the conference the child's learning (or lack thereof) rather than a discussion of the many points needed to make a grade. With their grades now determined by learning tied to specific objectives, the entire process of teaching and learning held so much more integrity for me, for the student, and for the parents, which opened up a whole new realm of communication in parent-teacher conferences.

Low-Performing Students

Let me write for a moment about the low-performing student who has been caught in a cycle of failure. Not only have that child's parents heard the same report from every teacher, but they have probably heard the same report year after year after year: "Lee won't turn in assignments and has numerous zeroes for late papers, and this has resulted in a lowering of his grade." Imagine the moment when these parents sit across from me: I show them a report that focuses on their child's demonstration of learning and explain that their child has earned a *C* or a *B*—or sometimes even an *A*.

The response from parents has certainly differed. Some have raised their lowered eyes and asked incredulously, "Are you *sure* this is Lee's grade?" Some have almost broken down in tears. Others have responded that their child "just likes your class." To which I invariably reply, "That cannot be. Remember, I teach history!" For the parents of high-performing students, the response to seeing the learning their children are demonstrating is no less enthusiastic.

I am struck by the reminder that every student who walks through my door is someone's Josh or Ellie. If, as educators, we know that there are certain methods proven to improve student achievement, and we refuse to make efforts to implement these changes in our own classrooms, are we not guilty of educational malpractice? Every child who passes through our doors deserves no less than our very best efforts; they are all equally deserving of lessons that pass the "Josh and Ellie test."

Learning Targets

The first tenet of the Big Four is to know and use clearly articulated learning targets that are robust concepts, generalizations, or procedures. Teachers can do this by

- Identifying "just-right" targets
- Understanding the difference between content and lifelong learning benchmarks
- Discriminating between declarative and procedural knowledge
- Meeting and exceeding state standards
- Ensuring the utility of the curriculum format
- Taking a systematic approach to the curriculum process

RANDY HAS BEEN TEACHING MUSIC IN HIS DISTRICT FOR FOUR YEARS. WHEN HIS SCHOOL called me in to work on instructional strategies with his grade-level team, I asked team members to choose one unit they teach and identify the grade-level benchmarks or learning targets for that unit. My goal was to demonstrate how using benchmark statements as expectations for student performance would allow them to deliberately plan lessons to teach the knowledge or skills those statements identified. Randy stated that in his subject area—music—they did not have any learning objectives. (He added that the department chair believed that every teacher should maintain the autonomy to create his or her own curriculum.) With no set learning objectives for the fine arts, Randy deferred to the math teachers on the team to provide the information I requested.

Forty-five minutes and a call to the central office later, the math teachers produced not one, but *four* versions of their math standards and benchmarks. One version, a teacher explained with a rueful smile, was created several years ago when the state mandated that they show evidence of a viable curriculum. The second and third versions were modifications of the first, with those modifications mostly involving format changes (e.g., one looked like a curriculum map on a long, fold-out sheet of paper). The fourth, identified by the district office as *the one,* was the most recent state version, downloaded and printed from the state Web site. This seemed like the most obvious starting place for our activity, but even so, the next steps weren't clear. This collection offered some specific grade-level standards, but it also included "clustered" grade documents (i.e., K–2, 3–5, 6–8, and 9–12) that didn't designate which student expectations belonged to which grade level. Furthermore, the state Web site made available some additional "suggested frameworks" for grade levels, along with some sample "assessment frameworks."

"Which ones are we supposed to use?" wondered Randy and his fellow teachers.

Does this sound familiar? It is a scene that plays out during the staff development days at countless schools across the country, and it's led many teachers to protest that they want to be curriculum *users,* not curriculum *writers.* Individual teachers should not be expected to hunt through piles of documents to cobble together the curriculum their students need. At the session I've described, one of Randy's colleagues declared that he didn't understand why someone couldn't just produce one set of standards for everyone. Another confessed that although it would be nice if they had the standards documents, there were so many other schoolwide initiatives to attend to that no one really had time to "do curriculum." In summary, many teachers appreciate a useful document that provides grade-level expectations but admit that they don't know how to produce curricula efficiently without revisiting the old "behavioral objective" days when teachers wrote curriculum over the course of two days, copied the resulting documents in a three-ring binder, and then put the binder on a shelf to gather dust.

Searching for Benjamin Bloom and the Useful Curriculum

In 1956, Benjamin Bloom insisted that the way to improve student learning was to give educators a classification system of educational objectives to promote the exchange of the best ideas and materials. Bloom and his colleagues believed that the *well-informed classroom teacher* would use the taxonomy as a guidepost for professional conversations. The conversations would lead to better teaching, better assessment, and better learning.

Since the 1950s, curriculum coordinators and teachers have searched for a classification system of educational objectives that would inform teachers and also positively affect student learning. Over the years, we have learned that when drafting learning targets (standards, benchmarks, and objectives), it's best to keep the following considerations in mind:

- The specificity of the benchmarks and objectives affects the results of student learning.
- A distinction should be made between content benchmarks and "lifelong learning" benchmarks.
- For instructional purposes, it is important to distinguish between declarative and procedural knowledge in benchmarks.
- It is prudent to align the documents to state assessments.

These factors support the utility of the curriculum document. What Randy— and all teachers—need are clear learning targets they can use not only to help plan instruction and assessment but also to share with students, so that students may track their progress toward meeting explicit levels of proficiency or performance.

"Just-Right" Targets

A "just-right" benchmark follows the Goldilocks rule: It is a statement that is not too broad, not too specific, but "just right." Understandably, a teacher might wonder if a benchmark isn't simply the same old objective or outcome with a new name. The answer is no. Hindsight tells us that outcomes were too broad and behavioral objectives too specific, but robust conceptual and procedural benchmarks are just right.

A standards-based curriculum connects each of the grade-level documents to one another by a common set of general statements—or standards—that define parameters of a subject area domain; the teacher's curriculum is a link in a chain connected by standards. Identifying standards, then, is the starting point in creating this chain. Fortunately, the Internet provides teachers with a range of sample standards documents. One useful site for finding up-to-date documents, Developing Educational Standards (http://edstandards.org/Standards.html#Subject), organizes standards documents by state and allows teachers to peruse various related sites as well. Teachers at American schools overseas may prefer to use the American Education Reaches Out (AERO) standards found at http://www.nesacenter.org/AERO.

Many of the online documents are organized by overarching K–12 subject area standards with various clusters (e.g., K–4, 5–8, 9–12) of benchmarks. Because the K–12 standards serve only as broad categories, teachers must "unpack" the standards to create local district benchmarks and then refine these further to create grade-level benchmarks. These benchmarks provide teachers with the goals articulated from earlier grade levels as well as those for later grade levels; they can be used for daily lesson and assessment planning. In Chapter 5, we will hear from an assistant superintendent who found that when teachers planned tasks to grade-level benchmarks but scored and gave feedback to students according to the more general standards, the students did not make the strong gains they did when teachers both planned tasks *and* scored and graded students to the benchmarks. We will also see that the data gleaned when teachers score students to benchmarks can be compiled under the category of a standard for ease of reporting.

In *Classroom Instruction That Works* (Marzano, Pickering, & Pollock, 2001), we wrote, "Research has consistently indicated that criterion-referenced feedback has a more powerful effect on student learning than norm-referenced feedback" (p. 98). From today's studies on improving performance in areas such as sports and fitness, we know that timely, individualized feedback based on explicit criteria is critical to boosting accomplishment. An unambiguous grade-level benchmark allows the teacher to give criterion-referenced feedback to the learner. When a student receives such feedback, he can make gains by obtaining more factual information, adding more practice, or applying more effort.

So, what does a "just-right" curriculum target look like? In language arts, a benchmark that is too broad might read like this: "Students will read, write, and speak about the purpose, structure, and elements of fiction or informational texts and provide evidence from those materials to support their understanding for various audiences." One that is too specific might read: "Identifies three main characters in a work of fiction." A just-right benchmark with specific content objectives might read: "Understands elements of character development (e.g., protagonist and antagonist; dynamic and static; traits and motivations; and stereotypes)." The benchmark states that the student should be able to understand the concept of character development, and the specific content objectives are examples or elements of that concept.

In social studies, a target that is too broad might read like this: "The student understands the shared ideals and diversity of American society and political culture." One that is too specific might read: "Recognizes famous Americans such as Martin Luther King Jr., Cesar Chavez, and Eleanor Roosevelt." And a just-right benchmark with specific content objectives might read: "Understands the changing lives of immigrants in American society during the post–Civil War period (e.g., factors that led to increased immigration from China, Ireland, and Germany; how immigrants adapted to daily life in the United States; and the changing roles of women due to the war)."

If the criterion is too general or broad, feedback will not be explicit enough for the learner to apply effort to make gains. Conversely, if the target is too specific, attainment may appear to be immediate but will likely be superficial and temporary. To gauge specificity, I recommend a strategy I call "Tab-on-the-Folder." Imagine a tab on a manila file folder. If the tab reads like the just-right immigration benchmark above, it's easy to imagine how the folder might be filled with organized facts about immigration and its effects (e.g., facts about the changes to women's roles in society brought about by immigration). Think about all that would have to fit in the too-broad "understands the shared ideals and diversity of American society and political culture." Now think about what would go in the too-narrow "recognizes famous Americans" folder.

As a teacher, I plan lesson activities so that the students learn different sets of related facts each day. In the past, I would have graded students on the isolated activities (worksheets, notes, homework), but I would not have deliberately demonstrated to the learners how those activities connected to a more general concept or principle—how they related to "the tab on the folder." Thus, students learned to ask for isolated grades on papers rather than tracking their conceptual understandings back to the benchmark. They were glad to get an 86 percent on a worksheet, even if they could not define "immigrant," use the concept to construct a new question, or recall the facts we'd discussed in class. Today, I would share the benchmarks and specific content objectives with the students and score each activity with a "benchmark" score (in addition to the number of right or wrong answers on the activity page) to help them connect the information to the tab on the folder. In Chapter 5 we will see how to keep records of benchmark scoring in a grade book.

Recent research on the ways humans remember information indicates that when one spends time steeped in facts about a topic, one organizes and reorganizes memory points to retrieve and use later in spontaneous, independent applications. Stated differently, when you read, hear, experience, or see information about a new topic, you will more likely be able to use that information independently if you apply a technique to rehearse it, such as taking notes, creating a nonlinguistic representation, or asking questions. In addition, deliberately referring back to the overarching concept (the benchmark—the tab on the folder) makes connections more useful, efficient, and memorable.

Lifelong Learning Benchmarks

In 1781, John Phillips, the founder of Phillips Exeter Academy, outlined the school's instructional mission like this: "Above all, it is expected that the attention of instructors to the disposition of the minds and morals of the youth under their charge will exceed every other care; well considering that though goodness without knowledge is weak and feeble, yet knowledge without goodness is dangerous, and that both united form the noblest character, and lay the surest foundation of usefulness to mankind." In these words, Phillips presents the rationale of establishing benchmarks outside of content areas.

Most curricula at the state or district level include benchmarks in knowledge or content areas, and students are taught and graded in these domains: mathematics, languages, science, social studies, physical education, practical arts, fine arts, and so on. Many schools also provide report card data about student performance in additional areas identified as "habits of mind" or study skills. At the elementary level, these assessments tend to constitute a separate cluster of grades, checkmarks, or comments; at the secondary level, they tend to be included in the subject-area grade.

John Koncki, a 6th grade teacher, explained in an e-mail to me that in order to give better feedback to his students, he separates his grades into content and noncontent categories:

> Based on middle school students' needs for improvement and capabilities, I separate the grades for communication (penmanship, neatness of presentation), character (participation, behavior, and attitude) and practice (homework). I want to be able to show effort and behavior apart from content knowledge, in science, for example. I weight these categories differently in final grades, but on daily performance they are now separated so the students see their discrete evaluations. The students need to see that their communication, character, and practice habits impact content understanding. In the past, when I did not provide the list of characteristics to the students and just factored these in the final grades, the students did not have the information they needed to make any attempt to improve. Now they do, but I had to create those categories and share them with the students.

Schools' approaches to addressing noncontent benchmarks vary widely, in part as a result of the outcomes decade, and a number of sources exist for finding these benchmarks or lifelong learning strategies. A teacher could begin with Arthur Costa and Bena Kallick's *Habits of Mind* book series (2000) or access any number of national counseling programs geared specifically toward improving nonacademic skills. Variations of criteria include communication, collaboration, thinking skills, and self-regulating behaviors.

There is some pedagogical confusion about this type of benchmark. Often, the work habit or study skill sections of report cards assess student performance even though in-class instruction does not support the improvement of these habits and skills. It makes sense that if one plans to score a student on a characteristic such as communication or collaboration, one should plan to deliberately teach the student various ways to improve upon that skill. In many schools, however, this is simply not the case.

Declarative and Procedural Knowledge

Although generations of teachers have intuitively known the difference between declarative knowledge (content mastery) and procedural knowledge (skill mastery), it's only recently that we have considered the value of identifying benchmarks and objectives as declarative and procedural in curriculum documents. In *Dimensions of Learning* (Marzano et al., 1992), we discussed the idea of identifying the types of knowledge for instructional purposes, but we didn't get into using the distinction as a characteristic for curriculum objectives. A few years later, in *A Comprehensive Guide to Designing Standards-Based Districts, Schools, and Classrooms* (1996), Robert Marzano and John Kendall introduced the first curriculum format to categorize curriculum statements as declarative and procedural knowledge.

In a curriculum document, the statements of declarative knowledge (facts, concepts, generalizations, and principles) are identified by the words *understands* or *knows*. The following examples demonstrate how this works for science, math, and geography statements:

The student
— Understands the effect of balanced and unbalanced forces on an object's motion. (Science)
— Understands and applies measures of central tendency, frequency, and distribution with rational numbers. (Math)
— Understands the ways people take aspects of the environment into account when deciding on locations for human activities. (Geography)

In each example, the word *understands* indicates declarative concepts and also provides the technical cue for the "verb ladder." The verb ladder refers to the progression from low-level verbs, such as *identify* or *describe,* up to the higher-level verbs, such as *analyze* or *synthesize,* which signal most of us to design lessons to "move up on Bloom's taxonomy." Teachers who use this format can read the declarative statement and decide for themselves which verb to use or, in other words, whether to have the students identify, describe, explain, solve a problem, compare, analyze, or apply information in a new situation. Using the verb-ladder approach, the benchmarks are the agreed-upon concepts or principles about the content, but the teacher has the flexibility to decide on the activity at the lesson design stage (see Chapter 3). This is a change from previous curriculum design formats, which directed teachers to write the objective statements with a presumption of activity, thereby limiting students to performing a very particular exercise designated by the "active verb" at the beginning of the objective statement.

Veteran teachers may remember the days of behavioral objective writing and the attendant admonition that "understanding" cannot be assessed. But in the verb ladder, *understands* and *knows* both serve as placeholders for active verbs, which translate into activities and experiences that help students organize declarative knowledge. If, however, the benchmark statement addresses procedural knowledge, the statement of student learning should begin with a verb that describes the steps that need to be practiced to attain automaticity, such as *add, compose, sing, draw,* or *graph.*

This simple distinction is critical because it enables a teacher to scan curriculum documents and gauge immediately which benchmarks will require students to organize facts and information (i.e., declarative statements that begin with *understands*) and which benchmarks will require tasks comprising extended repetition or practice (i.e., procedural statements that begin with other verbs).

How Many Benchmarks?

How many benchmarks should we have? The answer varies depending on the grade level and the subject area, but in general the feasible number of benchmarks reflects how much instruction and feedback the teacher can reasonably provide.

Although one could arguably arrive at a reasonable answer by figuring out how long learners need to be immersed in the content or calculating the number of days in the school year and dividing it by a desired number of benchmarks, my experience working with many teachers argues for avoiding set numbers and relying instead on common sense. Certainly, if you have 180 days in the school year, 180 benchmarks for a subject are too many, and 18 (10 days per benchmark) are too few. Most core subject area teachers in secondary schools find that having 40 to 45 benchmarks per grade level, per subject, is about right. At the primary level and secondary school applied arts areas, those numbers drop to about 25 per subject, per year. Generally, a teacher using the Big Four identifies the number of benchmarks according to what will realistically allow him to manage feedback and ensure positive changes in learning.

Format Makes a Difference

Technology has expanded our options when it comes to creating usable curricula. Many of us are familiar with the old curriculum format: a table with multiple columns representing goals, objectives, resources, and so on, usually featuring text so compressed by space constraints that it was difficult to read. Those documents served a purpose at the time but clearly lacked the flexibility that modern electronic media provide. Today, teachers can create and revise curriculum documents using scrollable electronic spreadsheets. They can e-mail their documents to colleagues or save the documents on a CD for physical dissemination. And they can post their curriculum to a Web site, either on their district's local intranet (giving immediate colleagues access) or on the Internet (allowing access to educators everywhere).

The electronic curriculum folder upholds the tenet that teachers need access to curriculum documents that are manageable and that transfer effortlessly to grade books. The curriculum folder on an intranet site may include components such as a department philosophy or syllabus in addition to the standards, benchmarks, maps, and unit plans. Figure 2.1 shows the various

---

FIGURE 2.1
Components of a Standards-Based Curriculum Guide

- Philosophy Document
- Syllabus or Course Description Document
- Standards for the Subject Area
- Grade-Level Benchmarks (SB)
- Grade-Level Benchmark and Specific Content (SBSC)
- Unit Titles or Projects *(may be changed yearly or by teacher choice.)*
- Unit Plans with Resources
- Unit/Project Planner with Lessons and Assessments

Source: Learning Horizon, Inc.

complementary documents that might make up a standards-based curriculum guide for each subject area. Let's take a closer look at some of these documents.

Philosophy Document

Subject area teachers (K–12) may write an instructional philosophy statement that shows an approach to teaching (e.g., process or reasoning strategies, or use of specialized equipment) otherwise not obvious in the standards.

Syllabus or Course Descriptions

These documents, most often used at the secondary level, describe a course with brief detail about the sequence of topics. They also frequently provide the course registration information.

Standards for the Subject Area

As described earlier in the section on just-right targets, a teacher can access a variety of standards documents, edit them to demonstrate the breadth of the content, and then begin the process of creating useful grade-level documents. In math, for example, a teacher might begin with his state K–12 standards and then find that to produce a workable version of these, he needs to modify or unpack them using other examples, such as the National Council of Teachers of Mathematics (NCTM) standards (available at www.nctm.org). Figure 2.2 offers an example of standards adapted for the Gunnison Community School in Colorado.

Grade-Level Standards and Benchmarks (SB) Documents

The grade-level teacher needs a single document containing the benchmarks for each content area. This critical document, called the SB (standards and benchmarks) document, serves as the base for tracking student progress by benchmarks. The SB document also provides the skeletal benchmarks for the cantilevered curriculum guide. Figure 2.3 shows a sample of an 8th grade English SB document from Baldwinsville, New York, compiled after using various state and national resources and further informed by training received for using 6 + 1 Trait Writing and the Big Six Information Literacy materials. It indicates a standard for gathering research information and the grade-level benchmarks.

FIGURE 2.2
Sample Math Standards

Standard 1:   Use number sense, numbers, and number relationships in problem-solving situations.

Standard 2:   Use algebraic methods to explore, model, and describe patterns and functions involving numbers, shapes, data, and graphs in problem-solving situations.

Standard 3:   Use data collection and analysis, statistics, and probability.

Standard 4:   Use geometric concepts, properties, and relationships in problem-solving situations.

Standard 5:   Use a variety of tools and techniques to measure and apply the results in problem-solving situations.

Standard 6.   Link concepts and procedures as they develop and use computational techniques (e.g., estimation, mental arithmetic, paper-and-pencil, calculators, and computers) in problem-solving situations.

Source: Gunnison Community School, Gunnison, Colorado. Aligned with the Colorado Department of Education Mathematics Standards (www.cde.state.co.us/) and the standards of the National Council of Teachers of Mathematics (www.nctm.org).

FIGURE 2.3
A Sample SB Document

Grade 8 Language Arts Standard 4

Knows how to search for and use information for research purposes.

LA8.4.1   Knows various strategies to generate ideas and define a research task.

LA8.4.2   Uses information-seeking strategies.

LA8.4.3   Uses a variety of resources to locate and access information to research a problem.

LA8.4.4   Organizes ideas from multiple sources in systematic ways.

LA8.4.5   Writes research in a synthesized and cohesive way.

LA8.4.6   Knows appropriate methods to cite and document reference sources.

LA8.4.7   Evaluates own work based on criteria for clear communication.

Source: Baldwinsville School District, Baldwinsville, New York. Aligned with the New York State Standards documents (www.emsc.nysed.gov), the K–12 Standards Compendium (www.mcrel.org), the Big 6 Information Literacy Skills (www.big6.com), and 6 + 1 Trait Writing (www.nwrel.org).

Standards, Benchmarks, and Specific Content (SBSC) Documents

A second format is the SBSC (standards, benchmarks, and specific content) document. The benchmarks are the same as those in the SB document, but this file acts as more of a curriculum guide because a teacher adds specific details. Depending on the teacher's preference, the SBSC can address daily objectives or lay out specific facts and strategies that elaborate on or provide examples of the conceptual or procedural benchmark. Figure 2.4 shows how one would expand Figure 2.3's example from an SB document to an SBSC document. Specific content objectives are identified as bullet points.

A word-processing trick one learns to employ is to create the SBSC document first, before the SB document. Once it is completed and saved, use the "Save As" function to save (and retitle) it as the SB document and then delete all of the bullet points.

Unit Title Documents

In some ways, a unit title document is the "map" of the school year. Most teachers already have a good idea of the units that they would like to teach,

---

FIGURE 2.4
A Sample SBSC Document

Grade 8 Language Arts Standard 4

Knows how to search for and use information for research purposes.

LA8.4.1 Knows various strategies to generate ideas and define a research task.
- Uses various questioning skills.
- Defines and redefines the research problem.

LA8.4.2 Uses information-seeking strategies.
- Identifies potential sources of information, print or nonprint, at school and at other locations.
- Evaluates information and information sources in order to reevaluate the research problem.
- Uses most important and relevant information to the research problem.
- Knows criteria for selecting sources to use or delete.
- Determines the appropriateness of an information source for a research topic.

Source: Baldwinsville School District, Baldwinsville, New York. Aligned with the New York State Learning Standards documents (www.emsc.nysed.gov), the K–12 Standards Compendium (www.mcrel.org), the Big 6 Information Literacy Skills (www.big6.com), and 6 + 1 Trait Writing (www.nwrel.org).

whether thematic (e.g., seasons, wars) or more content-specific (e.g., magnets, the Progressive era, tall tales, thumbnail sketches). Eighth grade English teacher Jeremy Cartier and his team plan using unit titles like these: "Autobiography/Biography," "Business Letter," "Grammar," "Holocaust," "Literary Terms," "Novel," "Poetry," and "Research Paper." Unit title documents can be merged to show a map of all of the titles for a grade level or across levels for a subject area.

Unit Plans

Finally, one "distributes" the benchmarks according to unit title. The most efficient way to do this is to open the SBSC grade-level document and use the "Save As" function to create a new file for each of the unit titles. The teacher decides which benchmarks to keep or delete from each of the units. At the end of the process, the teacher ends up with multiple "unit title" files, each containing a few critical benchmarks to teach and assess in that unit (see Figure 2.5, p. 42). To complete the unit plan, the teacher writes the available resources for the unit and, in some cases, adds a description of the assessments to be used. A second way to show the information is to organize the benchmarks by month, unit, or theme over the course of an entire school year. Figure 2.6 (pp. 45–46) shows an excerpt of one such chart, created by the 1st grade teachers at Reynolds Elementary School in Baldwinsville, New York.

At this point, the unit plan documents are ready for extended unit planning. This process incorporates the daily classroom lessons and assessments, and we'll look more closely at these elements in later chapters. The planning format I recommend has evolved based on need and simplicity of use. For teachers to work effectively—and work together—on curriculum development, they must have equal access to school computers. Unlimited shared access within and across grade levels to an electronic folder system allows teachers to discuss student performance based on the curriculum using a streamlined and uncomplicated procedure. The system's simplicity is key; most teachers can quickly learn how to access intranet folders and select the curriculum folder, the grade-level folder, or the unit planner document in order to begin designing lessons.

FIGURE 2.5

Benchmarks for a Unit Plan

Grade 6 Mathematics Unit: Measurement

Problem-Solving Strand

Standard 4: Students will monitor and reflect on the process of mathematical problem solving.

6.PS.17   Determine what information is needed to solve problem.
6.PS.21   Explain the methods and reasoning behind the problem-solving strategies used.
6.PS.23   Verify results of a problem.

Representation Strand

Standard 16: Students will create and use representations to organize, record, and communicate mathematical ideas.

6.R.1   Use physical objects, drawings, charts, tables, graphs, symbols, equations, or objects created using technology as representations.
6.R.3   Read, interpret, and extend external models.
6.R.4   Use standard and nonstandard representations with accuracy and detail.

Measurement Strand

Standard 29: Students will determine what can be measured and how, using appropriate methods and formulas.

Units of Measurement
6.M.1   Measure capacity and calculate volume of a rectangular prism.
6.M.2   Identify customary units of capacity (cups, pints, quarts, and gallons).
6.M.3   Identify equivalent customary units of capacity (cups to pints, pints to quarts, and quarts to gallons).
6.M.4   Identify metric units of capacity (liter and milliliter).
6.M.5   Identify equivalent metric units of capacity (milliliter to liter and liter to milliliter).
Tools and Methods
6.M.6   Determine the tool and technique to measure capacity with an appropriate level of precision.

Standard 32: Students will develop strategies for estimating measurements.

6.M.7   Estimate volume, area, and circumference.
6.M.8   Justify the reasonableness of estimates.
6.M.9   Determine personal references for capacity.

Source: Baldwinsville School District, Baldwinsville, New York. Aligned with New York State Learning Standards for Mathematics, Science, and Technology (www.emsc.nysed.gov/ciai/mst.html).

Ensuring Alignment to State Standards and Benchmarks

A teacher may be concerned about whether or not the benchmarks used in the classroom have to match the state standards and assessment frameworks. The answer is, "Yes, but . . ."

When creating curriculum documents, educators in any state can access state standards and benchmarks and assessment frameworks online. As noted, because many state standards documents are written at a very general level, it may be beneficial to "unpack" them using more specific information from a variety of sources: core curricula; national reports such as National Science Education Standards (NSES) or National Council for the Social Studies (NCSS) curriculum standards; the synthesis of national and international reports such as the Compendium of K–12 Standards (www.mcrel.org/standards-benchmarks) or the international AERO documents (www.ncsacenter.org/AERO); and any existing local curriculum documents.

When using the SB/SBSC process I've described to draft standards and create grade-level benchmarks, 6th grade teacher Emily Kowal color-codes her documents by indicating in blue the benchmarks that her state's assessment framework identifies as likely to be tested statewide. She uses black for the rest of the text, which shows the knowledge and skills she teaches and assesses but that are not necessarily tested on a state point-in-time assessment. Colorado State Assessment Coordinator Maria Bagby supports the idea of clearly indicating which benchmarks will be tested on state and classroom tests and which will be assessed through classroom tasks, and offers a clarification:

> We are a "local control" state—that is, in Colorado, each local board of education holds the responsibility of determining the curriculum of the students in the community. The state only requires that the local standards and curriculum we use align (in content, not format) with the Colorado Model Content Standards and CSAP (test) Assessment Objectives.

> One issue is the confusion about the difference between a state assessment (i.e., large-scale, standardized, timed, paper-pencil) and district and school-level curriculum. Many seem to be making the CSAP assessment frameworks a "de-facto curriculum." The assessment frameworks outline

FIGURE 2.6
Benchmarks for an Entire Year

Grade 1 English/Language Arts Curriculum Map for Reading

September	October	November	December	January
Harcourt Brace Book 1-1	Harcourt Brace Book 1-1	Harcourt Brace Book 1-2	Harcourt Brace Book 1-2	Harcourt Brace Book 1-3
LA1.5.2 Various strategies to aid comprehension:	**LA1.5.2** Various strategies to aid comprehension	**LA1.5.2** Various strategies to aid comprehension	**LA1.5.1** Concepts of print	**LA1.5.2** Various strategies to aid comprehension
• Sequencing • Drawing conclusions (pictures) • Self-correcting	• Sequencing • Drawing conclusions (pictures) • Self-correcting	• Identifying cause/effect • Visualizing • Sequencing • Summarizing	• Understanding use of capitalization and punctuation as text boundaries	• Predicting • Making inferences • Sequencing • Summarizing
LA1.5.3 Phonetic analysis	**LA1.5.3** Phonetic analysis	**LA1.5.3** Phonetic analysis	**LA1.5.2** Various strategies to aid comprehension	**LA1.5.3** Phonetic analysis
• Knows letters/sounds • Knows difference between vowels and consonants • Short vowels a and i • -ap, -at, -ill, -it	• Segments three phonemes • Rhyme • Short vowel o, variant o • Digraph ck, th, ch, wh, sh • ick, ink, all, ill	• Short vowel e and u • est, ent • s and rr blends • Digraph th	• Details • Reread aloud and LA 1.5.6 self-correct	• Digraphs ch, tch, qu, wh • Initial blends with i • ar
LA1.5.4 Structural analysis	**LA1.5.4** Structural analysis	**LA1.5.4** Structural analysis	**LA1.5.3** Phonetic analysis	**LA1.5.4** Structural analysis
• Contraction 's • Inflection -s	• Contraction n't		• Diphthong ng • r-controlled vowel • ang, ing • Digraph sh • Initial blends s/r • Consonant-vowel-consonant	• Inflections -ed, -ing • Chunking
	LA 1.5.5 Level-appropriate sight reading	**LA1.5.6** Self-correction strategies	**LA1.5.4** Structural analysis	**LA1.5.5** Level-appropriate sight reading
	• Dolch Set A • DRA Level 4 instructions	• Rereading	• Compound words • Chunking	• Dolch Sets A–C • DRA 8 instructions
	LA1.6.3 Simple inferences		**LA1.6.2** Story elements	**LA1.6.2** Story elements
	• Using prior knowledge and relating to personal experience		• Main ideas and details • Setting • Character	

FIGURE 2.6
Benchmarks for an Entire Year—*(continued)*

Grade 1 English/Language Arts Curriculum Map for Reading

February	March	April	May	June
Harcourt Brace Book 1-3	Harcourt Brace Book 1-4	Harcourt Brace Book 1-4	Harcourt Brace Book 1-5	Harcourt Brace Book 1-5
LA1.5.2 Various strategies to aid comprehension	**LA1.5.2** Various strategies to aid comprehension	**LA1.5.2** Various strategies to aid comprehension	**LA1.5.2** Various strategies to aid comprehension	**LA1.5.2** Various strategies to aid comprehension
• Reading ahead • Rereading • Predicting • Confirming • Telling fact from fiction	• Classifying • Categorizing • Alphabetizing • Sequencing • Summarizing • Predicting • Confirming	• Classifying • Categorizing • Alphabetizing • Visualizing • Rereading aloud • Reading ahead • Identifying cause/effect	• Identifying cause/effect • Identifying main idea • Reading ahead • Identifying plot	• Identifying plot • Making inferences • Predicting • Identifying main idea • Sequencing • Summarizing
LA1.5.3 Phonetic analysis	**LA1.5.3** Phonetic analysis	**LA1.5.3** Phonetic analysis	**LA1.5.3** Phonetic analysis	**LA1.5.3** Phonetic analysis
• er, ir, ur • -ie • ow, oa • Initial blend s/r	• Long e, ee, ea • Long a, bossy e, -ake, -ate, y = long i	• Long i • i-e,-ine, -ice, -ide, -own, -ound • Soft c • Variant ou/ow, y=long i, ie, long vowel o-e	• Long i, igh; long a, ai, ai, ay; long o • ail, ain	• Soft g (dge) • Long u, u-e; short e, ea, variant oo, -oom, -oot • -er, -est
LA1.5.4 Structural analysis	**LA1.5.4** Structural analysis	**LA1.5.4** Structural analysis	**LA1.5.4** Structural analysis	**LA1.5.4** Structural analysis
• Contractions 've, 're • Inflections -er , -est	• -ed, -ing • Contractions 's, n', 'll • Chunking	• Inflections -s, -ed, -ing • Contractions 's, n't, 'll, initial i blends	• Inflections -ed, -ing • Contractions 've, 'd, 're • Chunking	• Inflections -ed, -ing • Contractions 've, 'd, 're
	LA1.5.6 Self-correction strategies	**LA1.5.5** Reading level-appropriate sight words	**LA1.5.7** Reading aloud with fluency and expression	
		• Dolch sets A-E		
	LA1.5.7 Reading aloud with fluency and expression			

Source: Reynolds Elementary School, Baldwinsville, New York. Aligned with the Harcourt Brace Reading and Language Arts program *Trophies,* 2005 edition.

only what is possible to be measured on a three-hour, paper-and-pencil test, yet students need and deserve a curriculum that is rich with laboratory work and a rich curriculum that goes beyond what a three-hour, paper-and-pencil test is able to provide in education.

With the criteria for just-right benchmark and access to electronic resources, these Colorado teachers—and any teachers—can create useful, usable curriculum documents for their specific grade level or subject area. It is a matter of going to the state Web site to find the cluster grade-level documents; identifying those benchmarks that can be taught and assessed at the specific grade level; editing those benchmarks to align with the just-right criteria; and then beginning to deliberately teach, assess, and give feedback to learners. What makes the most sense is for teachers within a school to work on curriculum in subject area and grade-level teams so that they can create curriculum documents that provide both horizontal and vertical articulation. The remainder of this chapter assumes that teachers will collaborate to create curricula within an organization.

The Three- to Five-Year Plan

Historically, curriculum development took place over a seven-year cycle that emphasized a different subject area each year. During year one, the study year, teachers in a subject area would convene a committee to study the changes in the field. During year two, they would pilot any significant changes, which generally translated to using new textbooks in some classrooms. The committee would officially adopt new materials in year three, use the materials for the next few years and, finally, in the last year of the cycle, fill out evaluations recommending changes for the next cycle. Essentially, this process supported purchasing textbooks more than anything else; it was mostly a budget issue, in other words. The seven-year cycle allowed the time to rotate through subject areas in order to spread the cost of purchasing materials over several years. In many schools, the cycle eventually was shortened to five years, mainly to accommodate the technology or computer literacy changes of the 1980s and 1990s.

Taking into account available technology, the current recommendation for curriculum development is three to five years, with the process looking something like this:

• *Year One:* Teams in the core academic areas (i.e., language arts, math, science, social studies, and technology) draft curriculum documents and share and revise these documents electronically.

• *Year Two:* Core area teams begin to work on grading, record keeping, and scoring by the benchmarks, while teams in specialized areas (i.e., music, art, practical arts, and physical education) create, share, and revise their curriculum documents.

• *Year Three:* The core area teams work on unit and lesson design; the special area teams work on grading and record keeping; and the program areas (i.e., library, character education, and counseling) draft, share, and revise their curriculum documents.

• *Year Four:* The core area teams use data from scoring to make changes to benchmarks, while other area teams continue work on Years Two and Three tasks.

• *Year Five:* Necessary changes continue.

Because technology allows for immediate editing and communicating via e-mail or a network, changes to the curriculum documents can be made instantly, if necessary. In most cases, however, a curriculum committee must still consider the edits before final implementation.

There are five steps that can ensure a curriculum development process that is systematic, thorough, and accessible to various constituents. A curriculum supervisor can replicate these steps with subject areas in order to organize curriculum development on a very modest timeline and successfully communicate the process to the teachers, administrators, and community members.

Step 1: Make a Conceptual Timeline

Initially, the timeline serves the obvious purpose of identifying the sequence of steps required to work on documents. There are three useful types of timelines: a scrolling text version, a graphic representation, and a grid.

The benefit to using a scrolling-text conceptual timeline, such as the one in Figure 2.7, is versatility. It can be expanded to include further detail, such as meeting times and places, or edited down to its simplest form. Further, coordinators can revise meeting times with minimal effect on the rest of the file. This timeline is also easily e-mailed or posted and viewed on a district Web site.

A graphic representation conceptual timeline, such as the one in Figure 2.8 (p. 50), shows the stages of the curriculum process in a concise, visual format. This type of timeline lacks the detail of the text version but does provide the "big picture." Like the scrolling-text version, the graphic version can be easily modified as meeting dates or tasks change.

A grid-style conceptual timeline, such as the one in Figure 2.9 (p. 51), allows a school to track the progress teachers are making toward completion of the curriculum documents. This particular example was created by Layne Parmenter, principal of Urie Elementary School. He set up the matrix to show the content areas, the grade levels, and each teacher's name and the required documents. As teachers complete and submit each document, Layne highlights the matrix to keep track of their progress and also communicates with others by posting or e-mailing the matrix. Because the school district is small, the teachers have previously agreed-upon dates for completing the SB document, the SBSC document, the unit titles, and so on.

A curriculum coordinator might use combinations of the versions discussed here both to track the process and also communicate progress to teachers, administrators, and the board of education.

Step 2: Organize Meeting Times for Representatives

Foremost in setting meeting times is recognizing that teachers do not complete curriculum documents in one day. The curriculum coordinator can use either the condensed development model that John E. Gates used when he was director of the Escola Americana de Brasilia or the extended model used by Dawn Preston and her faculty at Baldwinsville School District in upstate New York.

For the condensed version, John identified four weeks in the school year when subsets of his staff would focus on the curriculum process. In October, English teachers were released for all or part of the week to work intensively on creating their documents. After an all-morning session addressing technical

FIGURE 2.7 **A Scrolling-Text Conceptual Timeline**		
Curriculum Work for the Spring Semester		
February		
February 9	Chemistry Physics Earth Science	8:00–10:45 a.m.
	Social Studies, Grades 9 and 11	12 noon–2:45 p.m.
	Languages Other Than English	2:45–3:45 p.m.
February 10	Art and Music, K–5	8:30–11:15 a.m.
	Curriculum Academy*	1:00–3:30 p.m.
March		
March 16	Elementary Science Curriculum Revision	8:30–11:15 a.m.
	Math–Algebra and Statistics	12 noon–2:45 p.m.
	Scoring Team A	2:45–3:45 p.m. Secondary 3:45–4:45 p.m. Elementary
March 17	High School Chemistry, Physics, Earth Science, and Special Ed. Team Leaders (a.m. only)	8:00 a.m.–2:45 p.m.
April		
April 19	High School Social Studies	8:00–10:45 a.m.
	High School Scoring Team English, Living Environment	12 noon–2:45 p.m.
	Curriculum Academy*	3:15–4:15 p.m.
April 20	K–8 Curriculum Revisions	8:00–10:45 a.m. (6–8) 8:30–11:15 a.m. (K–5)
	Math Documents TBA	12 noon–2:45 p.m.

* Including sessions for new teachers, principals, or other groups requesting additional time to review curriculum issues.

Source: Dawn Preston, Baldwinsville School District, Baldwinsville, New York.

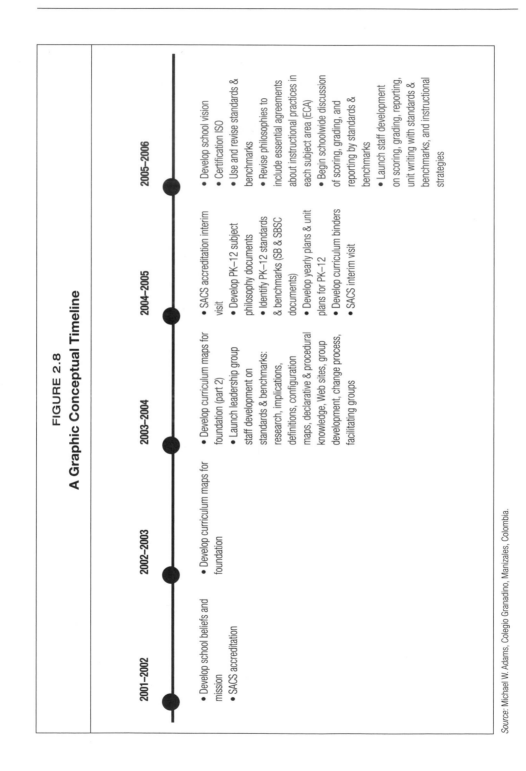

FIGURE 2.8
A Graphic Conceptual Timeline

2001–2002
- Develop school beliefs and mission
- SACS accreditation

2002–2003
- Develop curriculum maps for foundation

2003–2004
- Develop curriculum maps for foundation (part 2)
- Launch leadership group staff development on standards & benchmarks: research, implications, definitions, configuration maps, declarative & procedural knowledge, Web sites, group development, change process, facilitating groups

2004–2005
- SACS accreditation interim visit
- Develop PK–12 subject philosophy documents
- Identify PK–12 standards & benchmarks (SB & SBSC documents)
- Develop yearly plans & unit plans for PK–12
- Develop curriculum binders
- SACS interim visit

2005–2006
- Develop school vision
- Certification ISO
- Use and revise standards & benchmarks
- Revise philosophies to include essential agreements about instructional practices in each subject area (ECA)
- Begin schoolwide discussion of scoring, grading, and reporting by standards & benchmarks
- Launch staff development on scoring, grading, reporting, unit writing with standards & benchmarks, and instructional strategies

Source: Michael W. Adams, Colegio Granadino, Manizales, Colombia.

	FIGURE 2.9		
	A Grid-Style Conceptual Timeline		

Progress on Curriculum Document Development

Grade	Language Arts	Math	Science
K	*Sheila, Marsha* SB SBSC unit titles benchmark distribution	*Marsha* SB SBSC unit titles benchmark distribution	*Marsha* SB SBSC unit titles benchmark distribution
1	*Deann, Gwen* SB SBSC unit titles benchmark distribution	*Lil* SB SBSC unit titles benchmark distribution	*Lil* SB SBSC unit titles benchmark distribution
2	*Betty, Rita* SB SBSC benchmark check list	*Betty, ZoeAnne* SB SBSC unit titles benchmark distribution	*Rita* SB SBSC unit titles benchmark distribution
3	*Mike, Gordon* SB SBSC benchmark check list	*Mike, Gordon* SB SBSC unit titles benchmark distribution	*Mike, Gordon* SB SBSC unit titles benchmark distribution
4	*Mari* SB SBSC unit titles benchmark distribution	*Mari* SB SBSC unit titles benchmark distribution	*Mari* SB SBSC unit titles benchmark distribution

Source: Layne Parmenter, Urie Elementary School, Lyman, Wyoming.

aspects, such as the format and the revision process to create "scoreable targets," a teacher from each grade level sat at a computer side-by-side with teachers from other grade levels so they could talk while working. Typically, the primary teachers would complete their documents after a day and a half and could return to their classes. Intermediate grade teachers (grades 3–5) drafted their documents in about three days, and middle school teachers and high school teachers completed their documents in about four days.

Throughout the week, the teachers returned to their classes at special times or for specific tasks so as not to make the week too disruptive to their pedagogy or to student learning. Each afternoon, the teachers posted their files electronically, and each received a reminder e-mail prompting them to check the documents and e-mail any concerns or edits to the coordinator, especially as they related to existing programs. The fifth day of the week was reserved for the coordinator and the tech director to post documents for teachers to use either on the network or online.

The process is intense, but it works. At John's school, the other subject area teachers met in similar modules during the three remaining "curriculum weeks" over the course of the year. This week-long model can also be conducted during the summer rather than during the school year.

Assistant Superintendent Dawn Preston did not feel that the intensive, condensed model would work for her district because of the lack of substitute teacher availability. Still, by dedicating four or five days to the task, the Baldwinsville teachers were able to figure out when they could commit more days to the process and designate with whom they would work on those days (generally, they worked in groups set up by content area and grade level). With the assistance of tech support, they were able to post curriculum documents and complete them within a reasonable timeline.

Most curriculum coordinators prefer that the participants in the process include representation from all grade levels. Many have found success by organizing writing groups of grade-level representatives to draft the document, and then inviting the rest of the subject area's teachers to submit feedback and input through e-mail and intranet postings or in small-group meetings built into the regular school-day schedule or held after school.

Dawn Preston varied the process she used in her Baldwinsville schools to suit the teachers she worked with. As it turned out, the elementary and middle school teachers preferred to write their curriculum documents during the school year, whereas the high school teachers preferred to create their documents during summer curriculum sessions. In each case, Dawn adjusted the task completion timetable to accommodate the times the teachers believed they could do their best work and complete the revision process with colleagues.

Step 3: Choose a Format and Use Technology

A curriculum document format should be utilitarian first and foremost. Many school and state documents are expertly designed but cannot be shared electronically without losing formatting; this limits their usefulness. An uncomplicated Word file with few font variations suffices to provide the necessary information a teacher needs. What's more, simple Word files are easily edited. In some cases, curriculum coordinators keep the standards and benchmarks publicly available but password-protect other professional resources, such as unit planners and assessments. This is the approach taken by Phil Eickstaedt, director of standards and assessment for Oshkosh School District in Wisconsin. Phil maintains updated documents that teachers can access through the Internet and has found this to be a great way of maximizing the utility of curriculum documents while safeguarding critical information.

Currently, software programs exist to manage curriculum documents. A school or district can get similar results by placing folders on the school or district intranet and designating them as read-only to all but those teachers working on curriculum committees. Read-only format allows teachers to copy documents for classroom and daily use but not change the original files, either purposely or inadvertently.

Step 4: Consult Multiple Sources

When teachers create their curricula, they should access the leading curriculum resources. These include (1) previous school district curriculum documents; (2) national Web sites for subject areas, such as the National Council of Teachers of English (www.ncte.org), the synthesized version of national reports in the standards compendium available on the McREL Web site (www.mcrel. org), and frameworks for the National Assessment Governing Board (www. nagb.org); (3) international Web sites, for example, Ontario, Canada's curriculum (www.edu.gov.on.ca/eng/general/elemsec/elemsec.html); and (4) state documents, such as the California Content Standards (www.cde.ca.gov/be/

st/ss/index.asp), school district documents, and any material from programs teachers use for instruction.

In addition, many states provide assessment frameworks online that highlight specific criteria or content that will be included on the state tests. Teachers can use these frameworks to guide conversations about nonnegotiable benchmarks or specific content.

Step 5: Revise, Publish, and Use

Among the changes in the curriculum development process I follow now is that I take the time to give an overview of the Big Four at the beginning of a series of writing sessions, ask representative teachers to share the curriculum documents by e-mail or on the district Web site, and provide opportunities for teachers to continue to revise documents as they implement the benchmarks in instruction and assessment.

Technology permits teachers to update documents and gives them the ability to cut and paste the text into a variety of media: Web sites, spreadsheets, electronic task calendars, or handouts for students. Shelly Muza, a curriculum supervisor, notes the good news and bad news about electronic access and revision: "When teachers start using the SB and SBSC documents for lesson design and record keeping, they often recommend edits to the documents. They want to see the changes as soon as possible because they know that it adversely affects the learners when the benchmarks are not just right."

In summary, a teacher with a well-developed curriculum guide built on learning targets that are robust concepts, generalizations, or procedures can begin the process of planning instruction and assessment confident that what they do in the classroom *will* make a difference.

Teacher Voice

Michelle Crisafulli

Michelle is one of many teachers who worked in business before entering the teaching profession. As a 1st grade teacher listening to the discussion of the Big Four, Michelle became more and more passionate about how this approach could help her show her classroom "bottom line." Here, she discusses how, since she began to reorganize her class instruction and scoring, she has developed an affinity for sharing with other teachers beyond her grade level. The Big Four has given her the technical language she needed to do as Benjamin Bloom suggested: communicate with colleagues about student learning.

I ALWAYS THOUGHT OF MYSELF AS A PRETTY GOOD TEACHER. I HAD ENTERED THE PROFESSION at a later age, after nearly 10 successful years in corporate America followed by a period as a stay-at-home-mom to my now-teenage daughter. So, I came to teaching energized and excited, knowing that children can and do learn, and confident in my ability to influence that. And because of my goal-oriented (some might say Type A) personality and my past success in the business world, I was sure I could do well.

I was hired in a large, middle-class, suburban district immediately after finishing my master's degree in literacy. It was the very same district that had educated me. This, in and of itself, drove me to my highest level of commitment and performance, and I soon began to see what I thought were the hallmarks of being an effective teacher: positive feedback from my superiors, peers seeking my guidance, collaboration with other respected professionals, happy families, and children who liked coming to school and being in my class. But

I was plagued with the notion of "proof." I thought I was a good teacher, but how did I know for sure? I had no proof.

Nonetheless, I felt sure of my teaching abilities. Riding this wave of high self-esteem, I pursued National Board Certification. This, I reasoned, would prove to me and to everyone else my effectiveness as a teacher. I completed my work for certification in March of 2002 and waited until Thanksgiving weekend for the results. The news was bad: I had not achieved the necessary score. Disappointed, but believing that it must have been a fluke, I submitted a section for reconsideration in January of 2003. Then I endured another long wait only to receive the same result. My belief that I was a good teacher began to falter; I could not prove that I was good, so I must not be.

In business, I could prove how good I was by the profit that I generated month to month, which improved the bottom line of the corporation. My results were clear and simple and justified my existence in that company. Education, I quickly learned, had no way of giving me that kind of feedback. No elementary teachers with whom I worked or talked really knew how effective they were, except for *maybe* through the limited indicators provided by standardized test scores. Because there seemed no way to measure my efficacy, in my mind, there was no way to measure student learning and achievement. They were the same thing. These revelations were frustrating and demoralizing.

And then our district began looking at our curriculum—standards, benchmarks, record keeping, feedback, instruction, and assessment. It seemed like a whirlwind of change was upon us. We were introduced to a new district consultant, Janie Pollock. I knew from my previous staff development work and professional reading that she was an educator who could back up what she said with science. Finally, proof! This was what I had been looking for.

Janie introduced us to the Big Four. I remember it vividly. In the sunken library of our district's middle school, on a hot summer day, just one day after the school year had ended, she asserted that a teacher can do four things to improve student achievement measurably. And, she said, one teacher can make the difference—one teacher at a time. Those were her exact words. Score! This was where I was going to find my proof.

I have incorporated the Big Four into my learning world: my classroom. So, where is the proof of my own efficacy that I was so desperate to find? I have it every day. Not only do I have it, but I can also show it to anyone who's interested. More important than what I have taught, *I can show what my students know*. And I know they know it, because I measure it. I teach to the standards through benchmarks and specific content, and then I give my students lots of time and opportunities to practice and apply those concepts as I give them specific feedback about their proficiency. They get to practice and apply some more, and along the way, I am assessing and documenting their progress.

Further proof of learning is my 1st graders' ability to use what they have learned as a scaffold for new learning. For example, in the first month of the new school year, I decided to instruct and assess the names of the vowels. In the following month, my students were accountable for the sounds of those vowels in isolation. Logically, they were later expected to be able to apply their understanding of vowels in their reading and writing. Every single one of my students can do this.

The learning is visible. It's measurable. It's proof that all students in my class are learning the concepts and skills that our curriculum documents have laid out for them. Furthermore, my students are aware of their own learning and where they are falling short. With specific feedback, I help them close the gap on what they don't know but want to know.

In turn, I know that I am still closing my gap on student achievement. I have begun informally mentoring other teachers on using the Big Four, asking for feedback about my planning, instruction, and assessment from my colleagues. I have focused my participation in district activities outside the classroom on those that help me deepen my understanding and application of the Big Four. Now that I see results in student achievement, positive or negative, I can make tangible, measurable adjustments to my teaching. Student achievement happens not in spite of my instruction but because of it.

I need to tell you about a particular student—let's call him Jarrett. He was an adorable little boy with a December birthday, making him a little younger than many of his classmates. Before he joined my class, he had gone to a half-day kindergarten program, where he had struggled to learn letters, sounds, and numbers. His parents had him tutored during the summer between kindergarten and 1st grade. According to his tutor, Jarrett just couldn't seem to get the concept of letters and words. His parents indicated that they wanted him kept in kindergarten for two years because of his age and the difficulty he had learning basic language arts concepts.

My early testing of Jarrett supported the concerns of all the people who had worked with him prior to 1st grade. He scored significantly below average on our 1st grade screening and below average in a dictation assessment. This meant he knew only about half the letter names, very few sounds, and absolutely no words. Jarrett could write his name only by copying it from the nametag on his desk. This child was confused about text! The literacy teacher and I set out on a mission. We would hold him to the same benchmarks as every other student. We would instruct, assess, and provide specific feedback to him, to his parents, and to each other, and we would record his progress ferociously.

Today, Jarrett knows all his letters, can distinguish whether they are vowels or consonants, and can create the sounds letters make in isolation and in context while he is reading. He is reading instructionally at a DRA Level 3. When writing, he uses beginning, middle, and ending sounds, often using correct vowel sounds. This is not a child who had to stay in kindergarten to learn what he needed to know and be able to do. When I go back to my record-keeping documents and look at his progress, I see proof of improved student achievement.

What a fabulous thing it is for a teacher to know that she is doing a good job. To be sure that students are learning what they need to know is rewarding and inspiring. And I can prove it!

3

Instructional Planning and Delivery

The second tenet of the Big Four is to plan and use instructional strategies that help the learner remember and apply information and skills, not just do schoolwork. Teachers can do this by

- Familiarizing themselves with teaching schema history
- Understanding and using the Teaching Schema for Master Learners (TSML)
- Applying research on instructional strategies
- Incorporating the TSML into daily plan books
- Planning units with both the schema and just-right targets in mind

ASK A GROUP OF CLASSROOM TEACHERS ABOUT PLANNING LESSONS OR USING A TEACHING schema, and you'll likely get a variety of answers: "I'm a veteran staff member; I don't think I have a schema. I just do what I've always done. Sometimes I change it." "I think I plan for activities first. Sometimes I know what activity works best in a unit, so I just make sure I plan enough time so it can be finished at school." "I don't plan, per se. I look at where the students are each day and take them to the next step."

Many new teachers tell me that during their college experience, they learned lesson design by using Madeline Hunter's mastery teaching schema. Perhaps because of their inexperience and their limited exposure to the schema, they remember the task as something difficult and tedious. They tell me that using Hunter's schema to write one comprehensive lesson plan, as required in their lesson design course, was hard enough; designing *all* their lessons with such thoroughness seems downright unreasonable, and most admit that they are not inclined to do it once they leave the university class. When pressed to explain how they are planning for lessons, they quickly adopt the "activity planning" mentality of stringing together as many tasks as they can complete in a unit of study. Because this practice easily becomes habit, within months of landing their first teaching position, they find themselves in the same, entrenched-in-routine place as veteran teachers.

This leads us to pedagogical automaticity. Pedagogy, of course, is the study of teaching. Automaticity implies that the performance can be carried out without thinking about it. Together, the phrase refers to what teachers with an ingrained set of skills will be able to teach automatically, without needing to really think about what they are doing. It implies a state of fluidity and flexibility. For example, a teacher whose craft has reached the level of pedagogical automaticity could switch instructional strategies mid-class if she noted that the approach she'd planned was leading to student confusion. This teacher isn't thinking about her teaching as she delivers it; rather, she is automatically responding to her students' understandings and performances.

Many teachers say they teach with pedagogical automaticity, but for most of them, this translates to teaching on automatic pilot. When they notice that their students do not seem engaged with the content, they nevertheless continue to teach the lesson in the same way or attempt to modify their students' behavior with homework, quiet time, or a noninstructional measure. Remember, we inherited our pedagogical automaticity from the teachers we ourselves had in elementary and secondary school, so the problem often lies in the teaching habits that influence lesson planning.

Schema History

School improvement studies in the 1980s strongly associated high levels of student achievement with effective instructional planning and delivery. The terms *direct instruction* or *active teaching* were seen as important companions to the classroom management techniques thought to motivate and discipline students. Leading educators such as Barak Rosenshine, Jere Brophy, Robert Gagne, Beau Fly Jones, and Madeline Hunter proposed planning to deliver instruction in small steps, the better to present content to the students.

Planning for teaching dates to Johann F. Herbart (1776–1841), a German philosopher distinguished for developing a highly ordered mode of instruction that supported the idea that humankind could learn moral development with the right guidance (Ornstein & Levine, 1987). Herbart developed the doctrine of curriculum correlation that would become the foundation for modern curricula; it espoused the continuous integration of concepts in core areas, or a focus on the scope and sequence of content. The idea was to guide students through the academic process of acquiring knowledge in order to reach what Herbart called *apperception*. This system of education suggested that the learner would use the constant flow of ideas presented by the curriculum to generate and process new understandings; achieving that state of knowing and using information in an original way was the goal for all learners. *Apperception mass* would result from the retention, modification, combination, or elimination of existing ideas (Cooney, Cross, & Trunk, 1993). All this should sound familiar to educators who strive to reach the apex of Bloom's taxonomy in their classrooms.

Herbart's followers advocate five instructional steps:

1. *Prepare.* The teacher refers to materials learned earlier to stimulate the learner.

2. *Present.* The teacher presents new information to the students.

3. *Associate.* The teacher deliberately relates the new information to previously learned materials.

4. *Systematize.* The teacher gives examples of the generalizations or the principles to be learned by the students.

5. *Apply.* The students try the new materials or new ideas to demonstrate their personal mastery of knowledge.

Although the Herbart schema appears student-centered, it assumes that improving teaching will directly improve learning. Doubtless this is because in Herbart's time, universities organized teaching schools to research and provide practical skill sets for teachers. Herbart's ideas also led to the inclination for schools to organize the instructional component into arranged curricula of units and lessons. Later, educators such as John Dewey would eschew such preassembled instruction, but the practice nonetheless remains. Because Herbart passionately believed that the ultimate goal of education was to develop moral character in every student and that delinquency of thought or behavior was the direct result of a lack of suitable education, it is not surprising to find the vestiges of his work in more contemporary techniques for improving learning.

Many other educators and cognitive psychologists offered similar types of instructional guidelines. I'd like to highlight a few.

Events of Instruction

Robert Gagne (1965) proposed the adoption of nine instruction "events" similar in concept to the Hebartians' instruction steps:

1. Gain learners' attention.
2. Inform learners of the lesson objective.
3. Stimulate recall of previous learning.
4. Present stimulus material.
5. Provide learning guidance.
6. Elicit performance (i.e., practice).
7. Provide feedback.
8. Assess performance.
9. Enhance retention and transfer.

Lesson Components

Barak Rosenshine (1997) offered a comprehensive schema that he refers to as the Functions for Teaching Well-Structured Tasks. Rosenshine's schema consists of six steps and a series of sub-steps:

1. *Review.* Teachers review homework, relevant previous learning, and prerequisite skills and knowledge for upcoming lessons.

2. *Presentation.* Teachers state the lesson goals or provide an outline of those goals, present new material in small increments, model procedures, provide positive and negative examples of work, use clear language, check for student understanding, and avoid digressions.

3. *Guided practice.* Teachers employ a high frequency of questions, ensure that all students respond to the questions and receive feedback, and continue practice and questioning until students are fluent in the content.

4. *Corrections and feedback.* Teachers provide process feedback when answers are correct but hesitant, provide sustaining feedback and clues when answers are incorrect, and, finally, reteach material when necessary.

5. *Independent practice.* Teachers provide students with help or guidance for the initial steps, as well as active supervision where possible. Students continue practicing until their learning is automatic (where relevant) and routines are used to help slower students.

6. *Review.* Teachers conduct weekly and monthly reviews of students' learning.

Mastery Teaching

Madeline Hunter's planning method is probably the one that's most familiar to educators today. Published in her book *Mastery Teaching* (1982), Hunter's schema has been adapted to include a range of components. Here is the one common to most variations:

1. *Set the objective.* The teacher identifies what the students should learn.

2. *Anticipatory set.* The teacher uses a "hook" to grab the students' attention and put them in a learning frame of mind.

3. *Input and modeling.* The teacher presents information in the form of a lecture, film, or readings. The teacher presents a successful example of the product of the lesson.

4. *Checking for understanding and guided practice.* The teacher checks the students to make sure that they are "getting it." The teacher observes the students demonstrating their new learning and provides individual feedback.

5. *Independent practice.* The student applies the information.

The Teaching Schema for Master Learners

We talk about teaching our students to be ready for the 21st century, but how have we deliberately changed our pedagogy? Two noteworthy changes have occurred in the last 40 years that can positively affect the way teachers teach and learners learn. The first is the advent of the personal computer and the immediate availability of information and data. The second is the dramatic shift in psychological research from behaviorism to neuroscience. Any revisions to the teaching schema have to take these vital changes into account.

The uppermost change to our pedagogy is reflected in the schema's title. Hunter's schema (and, likewise, its title) assumed that if we focused on improving the teacher, the students would naturally improve. Although this may have worked prior to the shifting student population, that premise is no longer valid. One salient lesson we learned from the standards movement of the 1990s was that if we wanted to improve students, we had to make students—not the school, not the leadership, not the teachers—the focus of improvement. Therefore, the Teaching Schema for Master Learners (TSML) argues for teaching so that students learn to retain information for longer periods of time and can, consequently, remember and apply the information or the procedure.

Despite the need for major changes, there is much that was good about earlier teaching schemas. Successful previous elements were carried over, and the new schema eventually solidified into six basic steps, referred to with shorthand abbreviations:

1. Set the learning goal/benchmarks or objectives (GO).
2. Access prior knowledge (APK).
3. Acquire new information—declarative or procedural (NI).
4. Apply thinking skills or real-world situation (APP).
5. Generalize or summarize back to the objective/benchmark (GEN).
6. Assign homework, if necessary (HW).
* *The floating steps:* Feedback, feedback, feedback.

A teacher using the Teaching Schema for Master Learners designs lessons deliberately so as to prepare students for learning, help them connect new information to prior learning, and cement those ideas or skills. When the schema is used regularly for planning, it becomes automatic to think about teaching to the master learner.

Step 1: Set the Goal/Benchmark/Objective (GO)

In today's vernacular, the teacher identifies the conceptual benchmarks (declarative or procedural) for a lesson, along with specific daily content objectives.

For example, if the lesson addresses the science benchmark "Understands the complete mole concept and ways in which it can be used," then the specific content objectives might include actual mass versus relative mass, the relationship between the mole and the volume of a mole of molecules, or the relevance of molar volume and Avogadro's hypothesis. Although the teacher would likely teach to one benchmark for a number of days, the specific content objectives might vary from day to day.

In an elementary classroom, the benchmark might be "Understands how different community members take responsibility for the common good," and the daily objectives could involve studying different groups or individuals each day, such as politicians (e.g., mayor or governor), charities, and service workers (e.g., postal workers, firefighters, or librarians).

In *Classroom Instruction That Works* (Marzano et al., 2001), my colleagues and I identified goal setting and objective setting as important tools for directing feedback for improvement in the classroom. Without question, the teacher needs to establish the direction for learning or students will set their own, and it's unlikely their choice will have much to do with the lesson topic that day.

Step 2: Access Prior Knowledge (APK)

Hunter's intent for this step in the lesson planning process was clear, as was Herbart's. The latter wrote that the teacher should prepare or refer to earlier materials to stimulate the learner. Too often, however, teachers consider this part of the lesson a time to review homework or use an activity to get the student excited about learning. Frequently, the chosen activity does engage students but employs a gimmick or unrelated stimulus to do so. The actual goal is to provide stimulus that relates in some way to the lesson content. A teacher might think of the phrase "firing neurons" to characterize these first three to seven minutes of the lesson. Ideally, the teacher plans an activity, a question, or a demonstration to spur or fire activity in the student's neural network.

Consider what happens when I ask you to list all the words you associate with the word "cow." Immediately, your neurons fire, and you might say, "Milk, pastures, barn, hay, and moo." Now what happens if I ask you to list all the words you associate with the word "cambur"? Did you see pictures, think of smells, or hear anything, as you did with the prompt "cow"? Or did you draw a blank and then begin to try to figure out what the word might mean *to you*? (If you speak Spanish, "cambur" easily conjures the smells, colors, and sounds of the lush tropics and of a fruit: the banana.)

The beginning of the lesson should fire students' neurons in anticipation of the new information about to be learned; it should feel more like "cow" than "cambur" (unless, of course, you're in a Spanish class). In neurological terms, if the right neurons fire, then the information will "connect" and be more easily retrieved when you need it again. This step in lesson planning is hard to do!

One of my favorite APK stories describes one teacher's "K–W–L binge." Ricardo admitted that he had fallen into the habit of starting most lessons with an adaptation of Donna Ogle's K–W–L (what do you *know*, what do you *want to know*, what have you *learned*) strategy. It's a great strategy but not for every lesson. His use of this lesson opener had become so rote, Ricardo noted, that he would accept almost any answer from his students and move on. But he really wanted his students to be "fired up" about a new short story he was going to have them read. In the past, when introducing new stories, he had asked his students, "What do you already know about this author's style?" The response to this question had become more "cambur" than "cow," so Ricardo knew it was time to switch strategies.

Ricardo's new APK couldn't have been more different. One morning, his 9th graders bustled into the classroom and one called out, "Someone left a coat on my chair!" Another student answered, "The teachers meet in here, so just look through the pockets and find out the owner." The students quickly realized that various teachers had left their coats, and they all began rummaging through the pockets to identify the owners. Finding an assortment of items (all placed there by Ricardo), the students tried to deduce the owners of the coats. Ricardo pretended to be occupied long enough to let the students' curiosity take over. In mere minutes, they had become investigators predicting the coats' owners based on the evidence they'd culled from the pockets. Finally, Ricardo halted the activity, drawing them to the lesson of the day. "Leave the coats; I'll figure it out later when you are working on your assignment for the day. Let's turn to page 91 in your books." The class then read Jack Finney's short story "Contents of a Dead Man's Pockets."

As a practical note, many teachers engage the students in the APK activity before informing them of the benchmarks and objectives for the daily lesson, stating that it adds the element of "inquiry" necessary for many tasks.

One confusing issue is whether or not reviewing previous homework at the beginning of the lesson is enough to "fire neurons." Although David Berliner (1986) found that standard homework reviews were associated with higher achievement, the teachers he spoke with were divided as to whether these reviews were a useful means of informal assessment. He concluded that teachers have a better shot at improving the overall learning in the classroom if they approach homework review in a purposeful manner, with a clear idea of the activity's purpose.

Consider Meegan Healey, who used various classroom openings with her middle school special education students before realizing that her prompts were not helping the students access prior knowledge or giving her the informal assessment information she needed. To fix the problem, Meegan adjusted her APK activities and, as the students struggled, reminded herself that the step's purpose was to fire neurons, not to provide new information. She'd fill those gaps during the next part of the lesson.

Step 3: Acquire New Information (NI)

In earlier schemas, the authors recommended presenting new information but didn't make a distinction between declarative and procedural knowledge. A practical and useful revision includes deliberately planning for declarative (facts and information) and procedural (skills and processes) knowledge, taking into account that each one requires different activities to boost knowledge retention.

Students acquire new information through their senses—hearing, seeing, smelling, touching, and tasting. In school, students will most likely obtain new information from seeing (reading and viewing) or hearing (lecture or conversation), so at this juncture, teachers have permission to lecture. The most important consideration for planning to teach declarative or procedural knowledge is selecting the type of strategy the learner will use to retain the information. If Jeff Lee, a middle school art teacher, wants his students to acquire declarative knowledge about the materials and techniques used for making clay jewelry (rather than, say, silver or bead jewelry), then he might lecture on the facts or details about these materials (declarative), stopping intermittently for students to take notes about various types of materials used in jewelry making. In a different lesson, he might decide to have students learn the steps (procedural) in the jewelry-making process by watching a video demonstration of jewelry making, allowing various pauses for note taking and summarization of the steps in the process. Later, when the students receive the materials, they'll use the steps recorded in their notes and start to practice, melding the declarative and procedural knowledge they've gained.

If a student is learning a new procedure but does not need to spend much time with the relevant declarative knowledge, then the teacher might demonstrate the new information in small stages so that the student can try to use that information, receive any necessary correction on its use, and continue practicing. For example, when elementary school technology specialist Diane Quirk introduces students to spreadsheet management software, she demonstrates a function and allows time for the students to learn the step before continuing. Diane schedules time for students to systematically practice the steps they need to gain fluency in the software; in some cases, depending on the task and equipment required to do the task, she may assign such practice for homework.

Occasionally, a lesson might emphasize declarative or procedural knowledge exclusively, but usually lessons employ a combination of tasks.

Step 4: Apply Knowledge (APP)

Knowledge gains meaning if you can apply it again in a reliable and accurate way. And students need to be able to use the declarative and procedural knowledge they learn in school both in the classroom and in the "real world." When planning for the application of declarative knowledge, thinking skills (e.g., comparison, analysis, persuasion) can help the learner organize and reorganize facts, leading to longer retention of the information and requiring insight as to how to use the information in a constructive manner. Various frameworks for thinking skills are available both in print and online. Chapter 4 describes in detail one such framework for assessment, which can also be applied as a guide for instruction on thinking skills.

As for procedural knowledge, research shows it takes about 24 "practices" for someone to learn a new procedure to a level of competency (Marzano et al., 2001). After that, subsequent practices have much less impact; the learner likely needs either a new situation or new declarative knowledge to take the procedure to a more productive level. Although 24 sounds like an unreasonable number if you think about it in terms of separate days of schooling, in reality, it's manageable. Just remember the days when you taught your child to ride a bike. Although it might have seemed to take forever, after about seven tries, she was moving independently, if awkwardly. It took a few more trips around the block to shape the skill.

Step 5: Generalize or Summarize (GEN)

When I get together with a group of teachers, I sometimes ask them what kind of closure activities they use in their classrooms. One teacher might mimic yelling over the student voices, "And your homework is . . ." Yet another teacher might imitate the sound of the school bell. Closure is that time after new learning occurs when the learner reflects on or summarizes what she now knows about the benchmarks and objectives that she may not have known before the lesson. This active time for a learner should include writing to a prompt, sharing aloud with a partner, summarizing using a strategy, or briefly drawing a pictograph depicting the gist of the topic for that lesson. These three to seven minutes metaphorically "close the neurons" as the bookend to the neuron-firing APK activity at the beginning of the lesson.

Often, teachers misunderstand the importance of having students participate in the closure portion of the lesson; many teachers summarize in their own words what they've taught during the lesson. If the teacher summarizes, it's the teacher who gets the benefit of the closure exercise, not the students.

Recall a time when you attended a lecture or a keynote presentation. After the stimulating hour, the speaker predictably summarized her speech. During those final three to four minutes, what did you and the others in the audience do? You probably began to tidy up or collect your belongings—in other words, you began to tune out. The classroom is no different. The teacher who prompts students to think back to the objectives, either by creating generalizations or new questions to ponder, keeps learning active even to the last minute.

Many teachers ask whether or not generalizing or summarizing could occur in other parts of the lesson the way that feedback happens. The simple answer is yes. In fact, summarizing is a skill easily employed throughout the lesson.

Step 6: Homework (HW)

Homework is the way to extend the school day, if necessary. Teachers assign homework to broaden the scope of declarative or procedural knowledge for the learner. Completing relevant readings, taking notes, or creating a graphic organizer on the day's lesson can all be useful in accomplishing this extension of knowledge. The homework assignment can then be used the next day in school to add new information. Homework is also a useful tactic when students need unsupervised practice with procedural knowledge.

The Floating Steps: Feedback, Feedback, Feedback

Although not numbered in the core list of steps, the "floating steps" are no less important. If you examine the other authors' schemas, each has a step or two related to evaluation, assessment, or providing feedback, but this step usually occurs at the end of the lesson. The reality is, as soon as you set the objective for the class, the feedback process can begin.

Feedback should be directly related to the benchmarks and objectives for the day in order for the student to make improvements. Teachers who understand the importance of feedback to the learner vary the types of feedback (verbal and nonverbal or written), the voices of feedback (self-reflection, peer, and teacher), and the opportunities for or timeliness of feedback comments. The floating feedback steps, then, occur throughout each lesson.

Instructional Strategies

Although it is critical, familiarity with the Teaching Schema for Mastery Learning alone isn't enough; one also needs research-based instructional strategies. In *Classroom Instruction That Works* (Marzano et al., 2001), my colleagues and I identified nine broad teaching strategies that can help students learn and retain information. The strategies are organized in the book by the level of effect they showed on learners in studies, however, it is also useful to look at them in the practical way that we use instructional strategies in the classroom so that they become a natural part of one's pedagogical automaticity. Let's look at some ways to approach the schema, organized by step.

Step 1: GO. Setting the goals (benchmarks and objectives) for the lesson is a non-negotiable step. The benchmarks and objectives are ideally organized as part of the school district curriculum as described in Chapter 2.

Step 2: APK. Several instructional strategies work well for accessing prior knowledge: nonlinguistic representations, advance organizers, and cooperative learning, to name just a few.

Step 3: NI. Lecturing and having students read or view new information are acceptable approaches to presenting new information, but the important strategies are the ones that the learner uses to organize the information, such as note taking, using a thinking skill as a scaffold organizer, creating a graphic organizer using nonlinguistic representations, and questioning. Of course, the cooperative learning authors remind us that "two heads are better than one," so pair/sharing and other partnering strategies help with clarifying and acquiring new knowledge.

Step 4: APP. Applying declarative knowledge implies that the student will be able to generate an original use of the knowledge, so any of the thinking skills work here, such as comparing, analyzing a situation as a system, examining different points of view to make a generalization, making a decision in a simulation, and creating a robust analogy in order to deepen understanding of a topic.

I want to pause to note that many teachers admit that although they do ask students to use thinking skills, they do not deliberately teach the process of using such skills. For example, when 8th grade science teacher Jodie Jantz wanted her students to analyze perspectives about genetic engineering, she realized they first needed to practice the general analysis process. For procedural knowledge, the best strategy is to have students repeat the procedure until they achieve automaticity and then have them try to repeat the procedure in various different situations or environments.

Step 5: GEN. Generalizing or summarizing is a strategy that applies to this section, especially in conjunction with cooperative learning, nonlinguistic representations, and generating questions. When students have to summarize or generate a question as a summary, they are more likely to retain the information. Sometimes I refer to this section as "putting the tab on the folder." Again, if you think of the facts learned as part of a metaphorical folder in the learner's mind, the tab is the summary and it allows the student to more efficiently find the information later. The tab is synonymous with the conceptual benchmark; the daily objectives, then, are the facts in the folder.

Step 6: HW (if necessary). When teachers believe that students would benefit from more reading or practice, assigning homework allows them to work unsupervised. In most cases, the student needs to receive some sort of feedback on the assignment the next day. The can be done by keeping the homework connected to the following day of instruction either as part of a review or as a necessary part of the progressing lessons.

Getting the Lesson Plan on the Page

If you were to look at Gary Nunnally's plan book today, you might see the following encrypted notes:

B/obj: 3.2.4, 3.2.5, 6.7.2
APK: clipboard analogy—nonling cause/effect
NI: mini-lecture Reconstruction—Cornell notes
APP: Deduction Tree/group of 3/summary paragraph
NI: 6 mins video—stop/notes
APP: Ded. Tree/continue indep.
GEN: Pair/share. Generate two questions as summary
HW: Finish Ded. Tree with new prompt

Gary uses the schema both for planning and delivery. He plans thoughtfully but writes his plan notes in the shorthand, providing detail in word-processed directions or student handouts. When I observe Gary's class, I use the shorthand notes as a guide to let me know when he thinks the students should be "firing neurons," connecting new information, applying new information, and summarizing what they now know.

By contrast, teacher Michelle Crisafulli decided that a more expanded approach was what she needed. She recreated an electronic plan book in order to keep the schema an overt part of her weekly lessons. (See Figure 3.1, pp. 74–75.)

Unit Planning

Unit planning is the process of tying together a natural sequence of lessons. The SB, SBSC, unit title, and distribution curriculum documents (as described in Chapter 2) are created as part of the district or school curriculum development process, so the teacher can access the unit with the distributed benchmarks to begin the unit planning process.

The teacher begins with the benchmarks and determines the likely sequence in the unit, which generally lasts three or four weeks. Then, systematically determining what new information is needed on which day, the teacher begins the process of filling in the tasks using the schema for each of the days in the unit.

Planning is personal. Despite the current popularity of the phrase "backward design," my experience has been that some teachers like to start with designing the assessment tasks first, others like to start at the beginning of the unit and methodically plan day-to-day instruction, and some, like myself, start by plotting the thinking skills against the new information to be introduced and then fill in the daily schema.

If a teacher has access to a robust set of benchmarks and specific content objectives, identifying how many of those benchmarks or objectives will be dealt with during a given unit or day is the most precise way to "plan backwards." Further, starting the lesson knowing the criteria for mastery helps you make sharper assessments and give students better feedback. Simply put, it's a sound way to plan.

In the next two chapters we will discuss specifically how to plan to assess the benchmarks. It is useful to divide the discourse about assessment into two parts. The first aspect is designing assessment tasks to accompany instruction and addressing the related validity issues. The second is tackling specific grading and scoring strategies tied to reliability of data and report cards. Chapter 4 takes a look at assessment tasks for the classroom or common assessments designed to require the student to recall and apply knowledge. Chapter 5 discusses the particulars about documenting feedback to learners—what we will

FIGURE 3.1
A Template for an Electronic Plan Book

Monday	Tuesday	Wednesday
8:40–9:00 Arrival	8:40–9:00 Arrival	8:40–9:00 Arrival
9–9:30 Morning Meeting GO: APK: NI: APP: GEN:	**9–9:30 Morning Meeting** GO: APK: NI: APP: GEN:	**9–9:30 Morning Meeting** GO: APK: NI: APP: GEN:
9:30–10:30 Math Lesson # ☐ Homelink	**9:30–10:30 Math** Lesson # ☐ Homelink	**9:30–10:30 Math** Lesson # ☐ Homelink
10:30–11:00 Science/Social Studies GO: APK: NI: APP: GEN:	**10:30–11:00 Science/Social Studies** GO: APK: NI: APP: GEN:	**10:30–11:00 Science/Social Studies** GO: APK: NI: APP: GEN:
11:05–11:35 Lunch	**11:05–11:35 Lunch**	**11:05–11:35 Lunch**
11:35–12:00 Word Study Lesson/page #	**11:35–12:00 Word Study** Lesson/page #	**11:35–12:00 Word Study** Lesson/page #
12:00–12:25 Playtime	12:00–12:25 Playtime	12:00–12:25 Playtime
12:30–1:10 Specials	12:30–1:10 Specials	12:30–1:10 Specials
1:15–3:15 Language Arts **1:15–2:00 Guided Reading**	**1:15–3:15 Language Arts** **1:15–2:00 Guided Reading**	**1:15–3:15 Language Arts** **1:15–2:00 Guided Reading**

Group	Level	Skill/Strategy		Group	Level	Skill/Strategy		Group	Level	Skill/Strategy
1				1				1		
2				2				2		

Monday	Tuesday	Wednesday
2:00–2:30 Conferences	**2:00–2:30 Conferences**	**2:00–2:30 Conferences**
Group	Group	Group
2:15–2:25 Book Buddies **2:25–2:30 Literature Share**	**2:00–2:15 Independent Read** **2:15–2:25 Book Buddies** **2:25–2:30 Literature Share**	**2:15–2:25 Book Buddies** **2:25–2:30 Literature Share**
Group	Group	Group
2:30–3:15 Writing Workshop GO: APK: NI: APP: GEN:	**2:30–3:15 Writing Workshop** GO: APK: NI: APP: GEN:	**2:30–3:15 Writing Workshop** GO: APK: NI: APP: GEN:

Source: Michelle Crisafulli, Reynolds Elementary School, Baldwinsville, New York.

FIGURE 3.1		
A Template for an Electronic Plan Book—*(continued)*		
Thursday	**Friday**	**Notes**
8:40–9:00 Arrival	8:40–9:00 Arrival	
9:00–9:30 Morning Meeting **Literacy** GO: APK: NI: APP: GEN:	**9:00–9:30 Morning Meeting** **Literacy** GO: APK: NI: APP: GEN:	
9:30–10:30 Math ☐ Lesson # Homelink	**9:30–10:30 Math** ☐ Lesson # Homelink	
10:30–11:00 Science/Social Studies GO: APK: NI: APP: GEN:	**10:30–11:00 Science/Social Studies** GO: APK: NI: APP: GEN:	
11:05–11:35 Lunch	**11:05–11:35 Lunch**	**Meetings**
11:35–12:00 Word Study Lesson/page #	**11:35–12:00 Word Study** Lesson/page #	
12:00–12:25 Playtime	12:00–12:25 Playtime	**Newsletter Info**
12:30–1:10 Specials	12:30–1:10 Specials	
1:15–3:15 Language Arts **1:15–2:00 Literacy** GO: APK: NI: APP: GEN:	**1:15–3:15 Language Arts** **1:15–2:00 Guided Reading** Group / Level / Skill/Strategy 1 2	
2:00–2:15 Conferences Group	**2:00–2:15 Independent Read**	
2:00–2:15 Independent Read **2:15–2:25 Book Buddies** **2:25–2:30 Literature Share** Group	**2:15–2:25 Book Buddies** **2:25–2:30 Literature Share** Group	
2:30–3:15 Writing Workshop GO: APK: NI: APP: GEN:	**2:30–3:15 Writing Workshop** GO: APK: NI: APP: GEN:	

call *scoring by benchmarks*—using grading devices, such as rubrics, and communications documents, such as report cards.

Teacher Voice

Danny Neville

I met Danny when I taught a graduate class at the Columbus School in Medellin, Colombia; he seemed like one of those teachers who had it all. By all accounts, he communicated well with staff and parents, and his 4th grade students left his class well-prepared for the next level. What a surprise it was for me to learn that he had long operated with just a "piecemeal" planning process. Danny's experience with the Teaching Schema for Mastery Learning highlights just how important it is for even good teachers to learn new techniques. His message? We can always become better.

ONCE, THE TASK OF PLANNING MY LESSONS FOR THE CLASSROOM SEEMED UNCOMPLICATED and, quite frankly, simple. I was an organized person. I'd always been able to plan my own learning, so why would this be any different? Before I got my teaching job, I didn't spend much time thinking about how I would plan my lessons. Nor was I taught the value of planning or how to do it properly and effectively. Of course, I used the standard "lesson plan" template my university professors gave out when they asked to see one of our lesson plans, but we all know that the amount of time put into planning one of those lessons doesn't last long once we're in the classroom. That was my beginning.

Things changed quickly. When I got my own classroom, I soon realized that planning was actually one of the most important things I could do as a teacher. I began to play with different day-planning book formats, using generic ones, creating my own, and looking at examples from other teachers and on the Internet. My objective was to find a planning system that I liked and use it to record the subject area (math, language arts) and what we'd be doing (page and question numbers, book titles, and so on) in class. That approach helped me to be ready in terms of what subject I was teaching and the activity that the students would be doing, but it did not help me to teach, nor did it really help my students to learn.

Finally, I began to take planning more seriously—considering the curriculum, the needs of all of my students, the objective to be reached, and how I could provide my students with the feedback they needed to improve. My system of planning was piecemeal, with some aspects planned on paper and some in my head. Despite my efforts, I was discouraged with my planning process.

I discovered the solution to my problem in the Teaching Schema for Master Learners for planning lessons and units and its clear series of steps: Set the objective, access prior knowledge, introduce new information, apply the new information, generalize, and assign homework, if it is needed.

Setting the Goals (GO)

Obviously, I knew that a good lesson should always begin with a specific objective in mind. The problem with my planning and lesson introduction was that I had not been deliberate about referring to declarative or procedural benchmarks when introducing a lesson to my students. Often the objective of the lesson would be hidden within the activity, not showing itself until much later in the lesson progression. By adding specific benchmarks from our curriculum into my lesson plans and briefly discussing them with the students at the beginning of the lesson, I was making the task much more transparent. Both my students and I immediately became much more focused on what we needed to accomplish. I noted an overnight difference in the quality of learning my students were demonstrating, especially when I was providing feedback and assessing their work.

Although our curriculum is very specific, the language of the benchmarks can often be somewhat confusing, especially for my 4th grade students. I began to alter the language of the benchmarks slightly for my students, beginning my objective with more specific language. For example, I'd use *The objective of this lesson is to know . . .* (for declarative knowledge) and *The objective of this lesson is to be able to . . .* (for procedural knowledge). These statements helped my students to know what was expected of them, as well as whether we were learning about things that they needed to *know* or things that they needed to *do*. I cannot emphasize enough how important it is to distinguish between declarative and procedural knowledge.

Another important aspect of this objective-setting stage is the use of exemplars to show to students at the beginning of a lesson. I have found that for some types of activities, it is helpful to show students examples of other students' work. This is a very delicate part of my lesson planning, because I do not want to encourage students to copy the exemplars or stifle their creativity in presentation.

For example, if the application of the learning objective is to create bar graphs using specific data, exemplars have proven quite effective. Because our grading system is based on a four-point scale, I try to use a minimum of four examples, showing and discussing examples of Novice, Apprentice, Proficient, and Expert work. Showing students what each of those bar graphs looks like helps them to see, from the beginning, what they need to do in order to reach their objective. In other cases, I tend not to use exemplars. For example, if I write, "The objective of this lesson is to draw what I know about the setting of the Zuckerman farm after reading Chapter 12 of *Charlotte's Web*," I would like my students to come up with their own interpretation, using their own form of expression and demonstrating their understanding of the reading.

Accessing Prior Knowledge (APK)

The Teaching Schema for Master Learners notes that accessing prior knowledge before introducing new material is a courtesy to our students. That was a good way to describe it to me, because I unconsciously used to skip this part a lot. By asking the right questions, we allow students to fire neurons related to the new learning benchmark or objective and mentally prepare for the upcoming lesson. By accessing prior knowledge before introducing new material, students will be more focused on the topic, ready to make connections, and better able to retain new information.

New Information (NI)

With each lesson that we teach, one of our goals as teachers is to deliver new information to our students. Simply delivering new information, however, is not the final goal. We need to ensure that the new information is retained so that students can apply it.

Traditionally, in "the place called school," parents, teachers, administrators, and anyone else remotely interested in education have been concerned with test scores, whether directly or indirectly. Even today, this tendency continues to influence many of our educational practices. To ensure that our students are learning (and that our teachers are teaching), students' knowledge in specific subject areas is tested and compared with the scores of other students. Often this practice can lead to more importance being placed on the passing of a test than on whether students can actually understand, retain, and retrieve information after long periods, hence the "drill and practice" and memorization strategies that were (and, in some cases, continue to be) overused in schools.

In my planning, the items that I include in the "New Information" section are (1) the material that will be introduced; (2) page numbers, book titles, and resources; and (3) the learning strategy or organizational method that will be used. I've come to believe that to ensure that we are using a variety of effective teaching and learning strategies, teachers need to be intentionally and purposefully incorporating successful strategies into our planning schema on a regular basis.

One of the most important distinctions that can be made in deciding which learning strategy to use for a particular lesson is whether the new information being introduced is procedural or declarative. For students to learn procedural knowledge (for example, hitting a baseball correctly), they need to practice the skill over and over, using the correct procedural steps, until they achieve automaticity with the skill. If the new information is declarative in nature, however, the strategies used must foster organization of facts rather than repetition and memorization.

Applying the New Information (APP)

During the application stage of the lesson, students should be using thinking skills or procedural practice, depending on the type of knowledge that has been introduced. Within the lesson-planning schema, the specific skill or type of practice should be outlined.

During the application step of a declarative knowledge lesson, we need to consider which thinking skill will help our students to best retain and retrieve the information. If our goal is for students to understand the concept at a basic knowledge or comprehension level, we may wish to use strategies such as classifying the information into different categories. However, if our objective is for students to reach a more analytical understanding, strategies such as performing a system analysis or forming a hypothesis will be more effective.

The application process of procedural knowledge needs to be addressed in more practical ways. Repetition, breakdown of steps, and specific modeling and instruction will help students become more comfortable with procedures. Later, they will be better able to repeat the process accurately, and eventually, they won't need to think about the skill to perform a task. Typing practice is an example of a procedural application. When we first begin to type, each keystroke is very deliberate, and we find we need to make corrections. After much practice, however, we can use the skill of typing automatically to accomplish more declarative procedures, such as typing a paragraph or letter.

Summarizing and Generalizing (GEN)

This part of lesson planning is probably one of the most often overlooked. Summarizing the basic points of the lesson or making general statements regarding the learning that occurred is often left out, even though it may be one of the most powerful and integral parts of the learning process.

When students learn new information and then apply that knowledge in various ways, reflecting on their learning can help to synthesize and solidify their experience. This process can also help to label the neurological "folders" in their minds and provide powerful connections to previously learned knowledge. Some effective ways to accomplish this vital step include writing reflective journals about learning; providing specific examples, illustrations, or connections to the content; summarizing the information; and making generalizations about what was learned.

Looking Ahead

I have created a plan book that acts as a schedule, day planner, and lesson-planning tool. I can and do use it readily. Using the Teaching Schema for Mastery Learning has helped me to be more productive with my time in the classroom. I am a more efficient planner, spending my time clearly plotting the sequence, content, and follow-up of each lesson. Because I have been using this new planning system for only a short time, I intend to reassess my methods and format after three months. I will use the schema for an entire term, continually giving myself feedback on things that are working well and things I need to correct, and generating ideas about how my planning process can be improved in the future.

4

Varied Classroom Assessments

The fourth tenet of the Big Four is to use varied assessment strategies to provide feedback that helps the learner hit the learning targets. Teachers can do this by

• Defining assessment
• Testing and teaching for thinking
• Understanding and using the KCAASE assessment model
• Employing observation and self-assessment
• Understanding how the "floating steps" differ from rigorous assessment

NOT LONG AGO, I RECEIVED AN E-MAIL FROM A TEACHER WHO HAD ATTENDED ONE OF MY seminars. Mike Musil, a 9th grade language arts teacher in Nebraska, had a question:

> We've just gotten to the "Land of the Lotus Eaters" in *The Odyssey*. In my notes for the unit, I came across a reminder that read, "Commercials for Land of the Lotus Eaters." I was curious to know what you thought of an activity like this. I know I could use it to assess understanding, but is it "fluffy"? The reason I'm asking is that I feel like a lot of the so-called performance assessments I may have done in the past were, well, fluffy. For example, I would have kids be reporters at the Capulet Ball in *Romeo and Juliet*. We'd take a day or a day and a half to do the activity. I've stopped

doing it because it seemed to me to be too fluffy. Maybe having students create commercials is one of those?

Later, by phone, Mike described to me how engaging the reporters-at-the-ball task had seemed when he planned it; the results, he claimed, were disappointing because the high school students put tremendous effort into creating visuals and skits but demonstrated simplistic application of the literature. In the end, the activity just didn't assess what he had intended.

"That made me want to go back to a multiple-choice test," he moaned. "I had wanted to know that the students remembered important details about that scene in *Romeo and Juliet,* but I was also trying to give them an opportunity to show me that they could think about it in a different way. Does it make sense to you that I wanted them to think more deeply about the text? Maybe that is a cliché. Anyway, it didn't work." Mike lamented the attempts he had made to use alternative assessments that seemed interesting during planning but lacked rigor when completed.

Similarly, 1st grade teacher Michelle Crisafulli admitted that she wasn't sure why she continued with a longstanding habit of planning "pumpkin activities" in the fall. Was it just that she felt obligated to do *something* with the pumpkins that students collected during their annual field trip to a local farm? Michelle said, "I tried to justify weighing and measuring activities as assessing math benchmarks, but when our new math program provided better tasks for those skills, I realized that I was making up activities because I had pumpkins and not because we needed pumpkins as resources to help students think about information or practice skills to meet curricular benchmarks."

Defining Assessment

Both Mike and Michelle recognized that they planned and implemented what should have been good assessment tasks but were stymied by the student results. In one case, the results were mundane at best, and in the other, the teacher did not need the data from the task to demonstrate student performance or to justify more instruction. In short, the data were invalid or not useful to them.

I've found that when I get together with teachers and start to discuss assessment, many of us find ourselves using assessment- and evaluation-related terms very differently. Figure 4.1 (p. 86) shows a graphic display of terms related to assessment; it can serve as a helpful blueprint for discussing frustrations and ideas for action.

The assessment discussion naturally divides into two parts: addresses assessment tasks (external or classroom measures) and specific grading and record-keeping methods tied to student feedback or reporting. The classroom teacher can strongly affect the dichotomy of classroom tasks and external measures. To meet criteria for state tests, and even common assessments, he can proactively match his benchmarks to criteria provided by the testing organization, as discussed in Chapter 2. When he receives an item analysis or other report for his class, he can identify areas of concern by benchmark as they relate to content that can be tested on a point-in-time test. In one school district, we found that the English language arts state assessment for the 4th grade tested just one-third of the benchmarks. This certainly supports the argument for classroom assessment that meets and exceeds state assessment.

Most teachers associate classroom assessment strategies with the following categories: self-assessment, observation, selected-response testing (matching, true/false, fill-in-the-blank, multiple-choice), short answer, essay, and projects. Another way to view testing strategies is to regroup them into just three categories: (1) testing for recall, (2) testing for thinking, and (3) observation and self-assessment.

Just as the teacher decides what he needs to assess by employing his benchmarks and objectives, he decides how to efficiently gather data to make judgments on student performance before, during, and after instruction. To generalize but not delimit, assessing before instruction can be either a formal or informal assessment that is conducted to confirm teacher beliefs about student performance level and used as baseline data. Assessment during instruction often falls into the category of the "floating steps" discussed in Chapter 3—or checking for understanding, giving quizzes, and documenting observations. Assessment after instruction, the most common definition of assessment, requires the selected-response and constructed-response tests.

Most teachers are familiar with the auspicious and inauspicious rationale for using selected-response testing or testing for recall. The third tenet of the Big Four states that a teacher should vary assessment in order to provide better

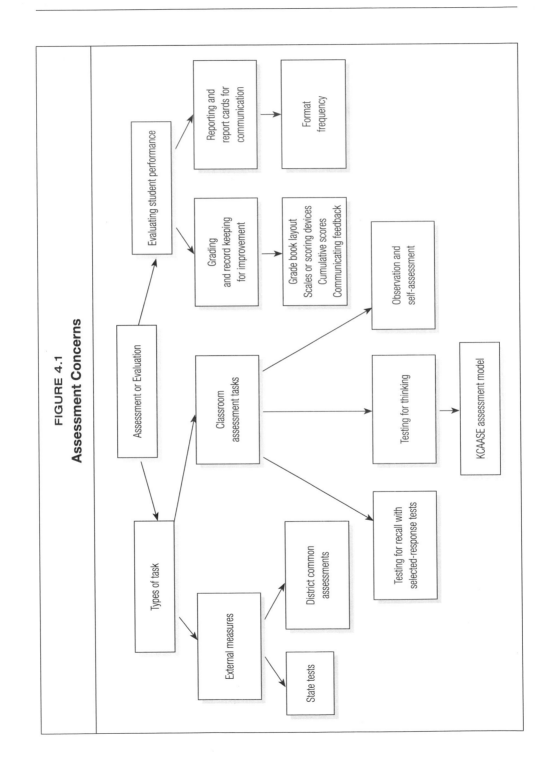

FIGURE 4.1
Assessment Concerns

feedback. To that end, we will discuss the first variation to selected-response assessments: testing thinking.

Testing and Teaching Thinking

Mike Musil remembers when he started creating assessments like the "Lotus Eaters" commercial; his principal had advised that he "vary the assessment" in his class. This might seem like a straightforward directive, but it's complicated by our past practices as teachers and the perceived purpose of testing. The directive to vary assessment implies that to assess knowledge, the teacher must do more than give "traditional" paper-and-pencil multiple-choice tests and worksheets. It implies that the teacher needs to assign tasks that require students to think for themselves, construct their own knowledge, and show that they can recall knowledge to use it in a meaningful way. So Mike, like many other teachers faced with the "vary assessment" dilemma, designed tasks based on performance and communication—skits, posters, commercials, physical models—that gave the pretense of better assessments but did not necessarily test thinking about the subject matter.

In the revised edition of the resource book for teaching thinking, *Developing Minds* (1991), Art Costa observes that much has had to happen in the field of cognitive sciences in order "for thinking to permeate the educational enterprise" (p. ix). The history of testing and teaching thinking skills is nothing new. Its august beginnings can be traced to the likes of Socrates and Aristotle. But since World War II, contemporary authors such as Matthew Lipman and Reuven Feuerstein have produced volumes of research, arguments, strategies, and admonitions about teaching students to think. By 1985, educators like Costa were arguing that if we wanted students to apply and construct knowledge, then tests or assessments needed to cue thinking. But obviously then, if we want students to think, we have to teach them how to do that. These days, to say that "much has happened in the field of neuroscience" constitutes a considerable understatement. Today, advocates of brain-based education, such as Pat Wolfe and Eric Jensen, provide the scientific basis for teaching thinking that was only in its infancy when Costa made his observation.

Mike Musil thought his nontraditional assessment tasks would prompt his students to think differently about the literature and demonstrate these insights through the assessments he'd designed. In retrospect, he realized that the students had done what he'd required (created skits), but they had not demonstrated recall and constructed a response to the text. Similar to using a schema for planning lessons, one can use a different schema for designing assessments that require thinking. Let's take a look at the steps to that end.

Back to the Future: Back to Benjamin Bloom

Although many excellent programs and classifications exist in print and online, we can return to Benjamin Bloom (1956), who urged us to apply the well-known taxonomy to testing procedures to determine "whether or not the student can remember and either cite or recognize accurate statements in response to particular questions, and also to use abstractions, display interactions, arrange patterns, use standards of appraisal [or critical evaluation], and evaluate selected or remembered materials" (p. 78).

Remember that in describing the taxonomy, Bloom and his colleagues wrote that testing knowledge alone constitutes only basic remembering, but the rest of the categories in the proposed taxonomy refer to using strategies that "emphasize the mental processes of organizing and reorganizing material to achieve a particular purpose" (p. 204).

Neurologists indicate that reorganizing information builds neural networks, which helps us remember more and construct new meanings from what we remember. Essential to our students is that they learn to organize and reorganize the information in the curriculum in order *to achieve a particular purpose.* That is the essential reason why we teach students to think.

In the business world, the term *situational cognition* describes the condition in which a worker is trained to be able to think spontaneously to meet company or consumer needs under new circumstances. In school, we can deliberately teach situational cognition by practicing and assessing thinking skills with the content of our curricular benchmarks and objectives. Students learn to think in schools, and because the process requires practice organizing and reorganizing facts and generalizations, they retain that information in order to use it.

Bloom's taxonomy provides a reliable structure to use for designing a situational cognition task. Remember the elements of the taxonomy: knowledge, comprehension, application, analysis, synthesis, and evaluation. Bloom and his colleagues offer examples of various types of thinking strategies for each of the broad categories. For example, in the category of knowledge, they state that the learner should recall specifics about people, places, and events, or even specific conventions or processes. In the area of comprehension, they recommend that the learner show the abilities to translate and extrapolate. In the category of synthesis, the authors write that the learner should independently make a plan or design a mode of communication.

As discussed in Chapter 3, the Teaching Schema for Master Learners includes a step on applying knowledge (APP). Providing opportunities for students to make multiple applications of declarative and procedural knowledge is one of the areas teachers tend to benignly overlook. When students learn procedural knowledge—writing, using computer software, physical movement, or even setting up a lab in chemistry or family consumer science class—they need to practice in order to become proficient; we test them by asking them to perform the procedures. Procedural knowledge is hard to learn, but also hard to forget, so assessments that take place after repetitions elicit accurate and valid data about the individual's performance.

Retaining declarative knowledge, including facts, concepts, and generalizations, poses a complex-thinking problem; in direct contrast to procedural knowledge, declarative knowledge is easy to learn and easy to forget. Historically, teachers have recommended memorization as a way to retain facts and generalizations to be followed by a test of discrete items. Well, all of us know that feeling of remembering information for a test only to forget it after a few days. More important, we know that when we memorize facts, we disregard deeply understanding the information. We memorize the knowledge for recall but aren't able to apply it to achieve a particular purpose at a later time.

Once one begins to think about the process of designing classroom assessments that require thinking, it's easy to see the connection between thinking skills in instruction and thinking skills in assessment; the boundaries often blur. In fact, I might have just as appropriately included this discussion about thinking skills in Chapter 3's discussion of the applying knowledge (APP) step in the Teaching Schema for Mastery Learners. I've often remarked that a teacher can design a task so that it requires students to think. If she gives feedback on the task and takes a grade or writes down a score, it is an assessment; if she prompts, gives feedback, and gives more information, it should be called instruction.

In keeping with the wisdom of the taxonomy but incorporating contemporary research, a teacher might consider using a classification system. Figure 4.2 shows an adaptation of Bloom's taxonomy incorporating strategies Robert J. Marzano, Debra J. Pickering, and I identified as powerful for student learning in *Classroom Instruction That Works* (2001). This is simply an interpretation to make the taxonomy more usable; a teacher might choose to use other strategies or even eschew the taxonomy provided by Bloom and his colleagues for another framework.

Each of the thinking skills in Bloom's taxonomy can be broken down into a defined set of steps that can be taught, practiced, and assessed in school. In a previous manual, *Dimensions of Learning* (Marzano et al., 1992), my colleagues and I synthesized the research and produced steps for many thinking skills

---

FIGURE 4.2
The KCAASE Assessment Method

Level of Thinking	Specific Thinking Skill
Knowledge	Recall by selected responses or cues (e.g., label, list, repeat, define)
Comprehension	Form a concept or convention Classify
Apply	Compare Make an analogy
Analyze	Examine points of view Explore a system or structure
Synthesize	Form and test hypotheses Persuade or argue
Evaluate	Make a judgment or critique Make a decision

based on the studies available at the time. Today, various sources in print and many sites on the Internet include steps for thinking skills. For example, the James Madison University Learning Toolbox Web site provides an approach to classifying that one might use to help students comprehend new information about a topic. This site (http://coe.jmu.edu/learningtoolbox/strategies.html) features a section on advanced thinking that includes acronyms for various thinking skills, of which CANDY is one:

C—Category title
A—Attributes of category members
N—Name all of the categories
D—Differentiate all of the category members
Y—You can draw the categories

Another site, EnglishBiz (www.englishbiz.co.uk), features useful strategies for writing or speaking to influence. It provides steps that differentiate argument and persuasion and examines the use of rhetorical devices. Yet another site, Write Design Online (www.writedesignonline.com), lays out various steps with organizers for use in comparison exercises. With a search of Internet resources, teachers like Mike and Michelle can create a thinking toolbox that includes the steps in the processes for each of the thinking skills. Many districts draft and adopt a set of thinking and reasoning skills that are employed as the process-learning benchmarks for highly declarative subject areas such as science, social studies, or art history.

Application of the KCAASE Assessment Model

Using the KCAASE model to design an assessment task is a five-step process:

1. Specify the benchmark(s) for the topic.
2. Select possible KCAASE thinking-skill levels and choose the preferred strategy for the task.
3. Refine the task with a situation or scenario.
4. Assign a communication device.
5. Make a scoring device, such as an analytic rubric, to give feedback on the procedure of thinking, the content or results of the thinking (the benchmark content), and communication.

Let's go through the process with Mike and see how he might use the KCAASE model to design an assessment task for his 9th graders studying *The Odyssey*:

1. *Mike specifies two benchmarks.* "Students understand the simple and complex actions between main and subordinate characters (e.g., internal and external conflicts)" and "Students know the archetypes and symbols used in the reading (e.g., supernatural helpers, banishment from an ideal world, the hero, beneficence of nature, dawn)."

2. *Mike decides he would like the students to analyze or evaluate the text.* To achieve this, he could brainstorm various sample tasks that would require the students to organize and reorganize specific facts about *The Odyssey* in order to better comprehend the conflicts and archetypes. They might analyze various points of view regarding the visit to the Land of the Lotus Eaters, or they might complete a decision-making tool to show the conflicting viewpoints.

3. *Mike writes about a situation culled from the reading that requires thinking.* "Odysseus wants to get home, but some of the sailors are weary of sailing. You have heard that there is a port nearby—the Land of the Lotus Eaters—that may be the perfect retreat. Complete a decision-making tree (such as the one described on www.mindtools.com/dectree.html) using accurate information from your text to show whether or not it is best to take a furlough."

4. *Mike's students work on his designated communication device.* In groups of three, they create a nonlinguistic representation of the decision-making tree to present to other students. After the presentations, each student writes an individual paragraph explaining the decision that he or she believes would be the best, using information from any of the presentations.

5. *Mike provides a scoring rubric for the steps in the thinking skill as well as for the mode of communication* (in this case, both nonlinguistic representation and a written piece). Students may use the scoring rubric to self-assess during the task development, during the presentation of the decision-making tree, and as a completion tool.

It is important to note that the thinking skill provides the scaffold that reveals the students' understandings of the benchmark to which they will be graded. The various steps and the conclusion provide the assessable information about the literary content. In this case, the decision is whether or not to stop at the island; this decision evolves to show one's understanding of the simple and complex actions between main and subordinate characters, using details from the text as examples. In this case, the protagonist's conflict with subordinates is the main deep understanding. This deep understanding takes shape as the students develop the decision-making tree; it would not take shape if the teacher chose, for example, to discuss the section on the Lotus Eaters and give students a fill-in-the-blank, 20-question test. By contrast, the decision-making assessment provides the opportunity, in the form of a situation, for students to demonstrate their recall of facts about the Lotus Eaters and Odysseus as well as their ability to reorganize those facts in order to make a decision.

Michelle's Pumpkins

Like Mike, Michelle Crisafulli was concerned about the value of her classroom activities. She sent me an e-mail describing her dilemma:

> Help! I have to do something different this year. Every year we go to the pumpkin patch and each of the 1st graders is given a pumpkin to bring back to the classroom. I set up activities in the classroom to measure and weigh pumpkins, count the lines of pumpkins, and make a class graph. In the past, I was motivated to change the activities because I was tired of the same ones year after year; I was in a serious "pedagogical automaticity rut." Now, I look at the pumpkin tasks as mostly busywork activities I had students doing because we had pumpkins. Our new math program is really good and has a lot of "real-world" activities, so this set of pumpkin-related tasks seems a waste of time, but I don't want to just send the pumpkins home.
>
> This year, I want to change the activity because (1) I'm not sure I honestly had a deliberate testing or instructional target; (2) I never really assessed or documented any of the conversations or observations about the students and their pumpkins as information about student performance; and (3) I'm not sure that the feedback that I gave to students was intended to help them improve as much as it was intended to praise them.

Michelle's assessment concerns differed from Mike's because she did have learning targets related to measurement and graphing (math) and comparing (science), even if she had not deliberately designed the pumpkin activities to gather those data. In effect, the students didn't really need to show her their skills in these areas because the math program provided the activities. Michelle insisted that having pumpkins did not enrich or enhance her existing math lessons; she wanted to instruct and assess to other benchmarks.

If Michelle decides on the benchmark to improve student use of descriptive language, then she could use the same assessment design steps. In the end, the task might be a synthesis task that requires 1st graders to persuade or argue a position. It might read like this: "Our principal needs help from the 1st graders! The display case in the front lobby of the school is empty and it is almost Parents Night. Let's persuade him to display the pumpkins that we brought back from the farm." With this task, the students would learn that using descriptive language when writing a letter to the principal makes the position they are taking stronger. Michelle would provide feedback to the learners for each step in the thinking process—in this case, persuasion—which allows them to extend their vocabulary.

If Michelle decides to revise the task as a science task, she might focus on the skill of generating hypotheses and zero-in on this benchmark: "Knows the basic needs of plants (e.g., air, water, nutrients, light)." To extend vocabulary and understanding of the benchmark, Michelle could design a task around the weight, size, and color of the pumpkins, as well as the students' recall of where they found them. She could create a conversation wherein students ask questions about the relationship between the sizes of the pumpkins and whether or not they received the same amounts of water or light, for example. Getting her students to ask questions is particularly important. Research shows that the average elementary teacher may ask as many as 348 questions a day (Sadker & Sadker, 1982), whereas the students may not ask any. During the discussion, Michelle might record scores for students' understanding of the material as well as their ability to generate questions or hypotheses.

I believe that any teacher who commits to testing for thinking is obliged to teach thinking. Fortunately, rewriting assessment tasks to include thinking skills naturally opens the door to restructuring instruction around a thinking skill. When assessing conceptual benchmarks, the teacher finds those benchmarks that lend themselves to thinking or constructing knowledge, rather than to simply recalling facts or steps in procedures. For some teachers, redesigning or varying assessments (the third tenet of the Big Four) around thinking spurs the need to improve lesson planning (the second tenet of the Big Four).

All subject areas require students to understand some declarative knowledge, so every subject area can benefit from assessment tasks that require thinking. Teachers in my workshops often relate stories of how the addition of these tasks has deepened their students' understanding. Art teacher Adriana Rocha described the varying techniques her students used to create their ceramics projects after she introduced a comparison matrix to analyze different ceramics techniques. Elementary teacher Mike Loria told of teaching and testing the skill for forming multiple hypotheses about why different kinds of birds have differently shaped beaks. He mused, "I never thought primary students could think and articulate such details of science. In the past, they only drew the different beak adaptations and matched them to the name of the adaptation." Middle school teacher Diane Clement related how she used an analogy to scuba diving instruction to help her students understand the critical role that feedback plays in their performance, or what she calls the "life and death of learning information in 6th grade." In each case, the individual classroom teacher committed to varying the assessment tasks by committing to testing for thinking skills and teaching students to use these skills.

Observation and Self-Assessment

Observation and self-assessment are two areas of assessment worth noting because they straddle the issues of designing assessment tasks and scoring by benchmarks. Although many elementary teachers use observation as a preferred assessment methodology, they confess to "keeping the data in their heads." One key change to the method is to translate these mental data into a more tangible form.

Each day, as part of his regular language arts instruction, elementary teacher Conway Chewning used to write one or two daily oral language (DOL) sentences on the board. These sentences included deliberate grammatical mistakes, which the students were expected to correct. While Conway walked around the room, the students finished the grammar corrections independently. When all the students had finished, Conway corrected the sentences on the board; the students corrected their own answers and turned them in to Conway. Then the class moved on. Honestly, Conway admitted, he didn't really consider this DOL activity as an assessment or a source of data; to him, it was just practice and his observations were informal.

We set out to revise Conway's DOL task. He was able to identify 10 characteristics of grammar (based on three benchmarks) he might assess by walking around and occasionally asking questions. His clipboard page listed student names vertically and the benchmarks horizontally. He was surprised at the richness of the data he could collect using only a simple, 3-point scale (3 = proficient, 2 = basic, 1 = needs prompting). After a couple of days of tracking performance scores during his usual walk-around, Conway found that he needed to be more deliberate in the choice of sentences he offered for correction. In a week, he felt confident about his knowledge of the students' performance levels and was able to start using the charts to show students where they needed to practice. The DOL activity was no longer just practice; because Conway used the curriculum criteria, it had become an important informal assessment tool.

Secondary teachers tend to minimize observation as an assessment methodology, but they can expect it to yield the same kind of gains that Conway experienced, provided they keep the first of the Big Four in mind and make sure they're assessing to quality targets. For some teachers, the informality of paper-and-pencil forms on a clipboard works for data collection. Other teachers find technology, such as PDAs, useful because it allows them to record data that can be transferred to a grade book at a later time.

The strategy of self-assessment is a constant footnote in the literature on assessment. Teachers like Gary Nunnally and physics teacher Stephen Rule found that giving students benchmarks at the beginning of the year or unit and then instructing them on how to self-assess and record these data in classroom notebooks resulted in both teachers and students having more confidence in the reliability of data about the students' performances. In the next chapter, we will discuss self-assessment and look at some examples of how students can track themselves using benchmarks, note their patterns of performance, and improve.

The Floating Feedback Steps versus Assessment

Before concluding this chapter, we need to revisit the Teaching Schema for Master Learners. When designing lessons or a unit, it's ideal to include thinking skills as the instructional tools in the "applying" step of the schema. Any time a student is asked to apply the new information is an opportunity for assessment. When designing an assessment, then, it naturally follows that one could incorporate the thinking skills in the questions, cues, or project directions. In addition, the schema's "floating steps" are meant to be the necessary but sometimes unplanned prompts a teacher provides to a student during instruction to improve that student's performance. This step is not intended to supplant rigorous assessment methodology.

In summary, one aspect of varying assessment is deliberately teaching and testing for thinking. In the days when learning targets were discrete objectives, selected response or recall strategies worked well to identify levels of student work. Today, when our just-right targets are more conceptual, teachers need to employ thinking skills to unravel information that the student has organized and retained. Further, informal self-assessment and observation techniques add to the body of evidence necessary for the teacher to truly know a student's level of performance and for the student to know his or her own level of performance in order to put forth the effort to improve.

Teacher Voice

Diane Quirk

Diane is an instructional technology resource teacher, and before she embraced the Big Four principles and the Teaching Schema for Master Learners, she found herself buried in teachers' requests for software and appeals for help with hardware. Now everything is different. As she explains, the Big Four approach has equipped her to dissect lessons and units to find out not only when teachers really need technology to improve student learning but also how that technology can best be incorporated to promote and assess thinking skills.

As an elementary classroom teacher, I spent many late nights creating a series of activities that my students would do when I had a class of my own. Eventually, my 1st graders got to experience the result of those late nights: my "apple unit," complete with poems, stories, songs, art projects, and much more. Looking back, I can't help but ask, *what was that all about?* We did activity after activity, and then—to end the unit—yet another activity on a much grander scale. I remember getting finished with that and wondering what my students had learned. At the time, we didn't have state standards, and we didn't have a written curriculum—at least not one that I could put my hands on. So, I just planned to teach what I thought they should learn.

When I left the classroom to assist in the implementation of the district's new technology plan, it became my job to train teachers to use technology in their lessons. My colleagues and I studied the relevant professional literature and recognized the phases that our fellow teachers would go through in the process of implementing technology. We tried to help them move through those phases, and we kept making adjustments to our training philosophy. We learned how to use the software and even began to demonstrate various classroom uses for it. For all this, though, we found that we ended up in the same place: still writing activities. The big difference was that our activities included the use of computers.

We tend to think that if a student is using a computer as part of an activity, then it's automatically a good activity. After all, they're using technology! But when we look at the results of that time spent at the computer, we really should be asking ourselves, *how did this use of technology improve student learning?*

About five years ago, some of my coworkers and I began to study and talk about thinking skills and performance assessments. We began to realize that we, as teachers, tend to be activity designers. Moreover, we tend to extend that "activity mentality" into the design of our assessments, which then just become extensions of activities—modified activities. If we focused instead on designing learning experiences purposefully built around thinking skills, then we could use those skills in assessments as well.

I've come to believe that students would benefit more if we moved away from teaching them *how to use technology* and toward teaching them *how to use technology to learn and think.* Adopting that philosophy would enable us to use technology to make a difference in student achievement, and I think that technology would more naturally flow from our curriculum benchmarks as a tool for learning.

When we look at examples of technology being used effectively in the classroom, we can see that it has the potential to empower student learning. We use technology to consume and produce *information,* to consume and produce *images,* to *interact* with others, and to assist us with *inquiry* or thinking skills. We have so many wonderful tools for doing all of this, and we haven't yet begun to fully tap into their ability to help students learn. Imagine how much richer and deeper student learning experiences would be if students could use technology effectively for these purposes. Imagine the depth of understanding that would result if students could use tools that would demonstrate their thinking or organize their thoughts, make better use of the tools available to access information and summarize it efficiently, create or find images that would reflect and support their thinking or understanding, and facilitate interaction with others who could provide differing points of view and unique perspectives. This approach would move us away from designing activities and bring us closer to providing genuine learning experiences that would improve student learning.

The best way I can think of to illustrate the difference between technology activities and technology learning experiences is to create some comparisons.

Kindergarten Activity: "We've been learning about the seasons of the year. When you go to the computer today, use the art tools to draw a picture of your favorite season, and then we'll print our pictures. During science, you'll share your picture with a buddy."

Kindergarten Learning Experience: "We've been learning about the seasons of the year. We used the Kidspiration software to help us to sort out pictures and think about how we compare animals, clothing, and weather for each of the four seasons. We've read library books about seasons, and we've watched videos to help us find more facts. Today, you're going to work in groups of four. Each of you will choose a season to illustrate using the software in KidPix. In your illustrations, show people and how they're dressed for that season and an activity that they might be doing, animals that you might see during that season, and what the weather looks like. You can go back to any of the information we've gathered and review it for ideas. When you've finished your work at the computer and printed your illustration, we'll work in our small groups again to explain what you've drawn and make some general statements about how each season is different and causes people to act differently." *(Technology for comparing)*

1st Grade Activity: "When you go to the computer today, I want you to think about what we've been learning about plants. Use KidPix to draw any kind of plant that we've studied, and we'll print these in color and post them on our bulletin board in the hallway."

1st Grade Learning Experience: "When you go to the computer today, I want you to think about what we've been learning about the parts of plants and what plants need to survive. We've located books in the library to help us find some facts. Today, we will visit various Web sites as a class so that we can see all kinds of plants and details about their various parts. There are also some video shots to show you what happens to plants when weather conditions change. You'll learn how plants react when it gets cold or dry and which parts are affected. Then, we'll make some predictions about what plants need to survive various conditions." *(Technology for systems analysis)*

3rd Grade Activity: "Today, you'll be reading some information that I found on the Time for Kids Web site about kids in different countries and what their day is like. When we meet for social studies this afternoon, I'd like you to share in a group discussion."

3rd Grade Learning Experience: "Today, you'll be using the Time for Kids Web site as another source of information in our study of cultures around the world. On this site, we can find information about a day in the life of kids in countries such as Kenya and Vietnam. As you take notes, you should pay attention to details about how they go to school, play, interact at home, and set goals. As a class, we'll create a set of prompts to analyze perspectives. The facts you find will help us determine how children in different cultures face similar issues." *(Technology for analyzing perspectives)*

5th Grade Activity: "Today, you're going to be doing an Internet scavenger hunt. I've located some Web sites about immigration for you, and you'll be going to those Web sites to answer some questions on the worksheet. When you've answered all the questions, I'll be looking to see that you've answered all of them with accuracy."

5th Grade Learning Experience: "During our unit on immigration, we've used the Library of Congress Web site to see photos and early films of various immigrants arriving in the United States at the turn of the 20th century. Now we are going to examine numbers of immigrants and try to identify patterns of settlement and assimilation. These other Web sites show the numbers of people who came from different countries and where they settled. After we take notes and graph the statistics, we will draw conclusions about the benefits of immigration and what patterns we are seeking today, in the early 21st century." *(Technology for information, images, and inquiry)*

Building Your Technological Toolbox

So, what do we need to do to move from using technology to using technology to learn? It's a pedagogical shift to go from designing activities with technology integrated for technology's sake to designing learning experiences with technology integrated to promote innovation and thinking.

Using technology for activities is essentially using a new tool to do the same old thing. In some cases, the teacher may teach only the functions of a software package and completely overlook how students might use the software's capabilities to truly unlock information and images that will allow them to study a topic deeply instead of using the limited information found in textbooks and other print resources. In contrast, using technology to promote thinking and support learning experiences allows teachers to guide, strengthen, and deepen understanding. It means building our own instructional toolbox where technology is used for information, images, interaction, and inquiry—to help students build a learning toolbox of their own for the same purposes. Once we can shift our thinking in that direction, we'll be closer to better instruction, better use of instructional strategies, better assessment tools, and better feedback to our students.

5

Feedback, Record Keeping, and Reporting

> The fourth and final tenet of the Big Four is to give methodical, criterion-based feedback to individual students. Teachers can do this by
>
> • Considering improvement versus assessment
> • Examining the "space" between the lesson plan and the recorded grade
> • Refocusing assessment and record keeping on benchmarks instead of activities
> • Giving timely verbal and written feedback
> • Using external measures

MY SON SAM, A 9TH GRADER, ASKED IF HIS REPORT CARD HAD ARRIVED IN THE MAIL. IT HAD. He found it and pored over it. Grinning, he said, "Here's what they say that I need to do to improve. Do you want to see it?"

I picked up the document, which was from the hockey camp where Sam had spent two weeks—the equivalent of 90 hours, or a semester's worth of class time. It described Sam's performance in eight broad categories of hockey (think "standards"). The first page was an executive summary with a chart that offered different scoring symbols (percentages, plus/minus, and raw scores), providing Sam with various ways to read and analyze his personal evaluation data. The multiple pages that followed presented approximately 10 specific performance statements per category (think "benchmarks") and also included scores. When Sam's score did not reach the benchmark for his age level, the section included statements about how to practice or make improvements.

I thought back to a few months earlier and the last school report card Sam had brought home. It never mentioned improvement; it didn't provide a list of skills and understandings for the subject areas with requisite scores indicating performance. Sam had barely glanced at that report card.

The Improvement Center

Is John Goodlad's place called school an "assessment center" or an "improvement center"? If it is an assessment center, the student tacitly acknowledges grades on a report card because these basically tell him where he falls on the normal curve. He is what he is. If school is an improvement center, however, then the student scrutinizes returned assignments and progress reports and finds information about areas where he could make gains.

In order for performance to accelerate or advance, one needs feedback on just-right criteria and the opportunity to apply or practice that performance again and again. Think about deciding to lose weight, save money, run a marathon, or meet some other personal goal. Research tells us that when someone makes a verbal New Year's resolution, the goal is generally dropped within three weeks. Various organizations recommend keeping written records of progress toward goals to use as personal feedback and using a buddy system or personal trainer. These approaches increase one's chances of hitting the mark because they ensure ongoing feedback.

In school, teachers give students verbal and written feedback and track their performances in grade books; this is all done in a sincere effort to help those students perform better. Teachers tell me that they give as much feedback as they perceive to be efficient and manageable. However, there are some common complicating factors. First, much of teachers' verbal feedback can be categorized as praise or behavior management; this type of feedback, directly addressing behavior, does not overtly guide students to improve upon curriculum targets. Second, producing written feedback is time-consuming. Given the rapid pace most teachers must maintain, it is difficult to provide written feedback within a time frame that will influence students' understanding of the curriculum target. The longer students must wait to receive feedback on a graded assignment, the more likely they are to see the returned assignment as "just a grade." They have learned to accept grades and often are surprised when a teacher suggests that they revise and resubmit work. And finally, most teachers' grade books are set up to track points for activities rather than levels of performance keyed to subject-area criteria or benchmarks.

This is the typical reality. Now, let's continue with a few general statements about what is possible:

• Most students can improve their performance on curriculum benchmarks and objectives if they receive prompt, criterion-referenced feedback.

• Teachers, peers, and the students themselves (through self-reflection) can generate this feedback during instructional time.

• Teachers can learn to score or evaluate student performance by the learning targets, give feedback to the learners, and track the data.

• Students can learn to track their own performances by benchmarks.

• Teachers and students can use these performance data in a strategic manner both to improve individual performance and to make overall program adjustments.

The Space in Between

Peggy Mihelich, a veteran 5th grade teacher, asks, "I understand that the tipping point for better learning is improving my verbal, written, and recorded feedback to students, but where do I start?"

It may sound a bit like taking the plunge down Alice's rabbit hole (and it will feel that way too, at least for a while), but a good place to start is by examining the "space" between planning the lesson and the grade that you enter on the report card. The space in between is your grade book and how you track student data.

I asked Peggy if she'd mind showing me her grade book. She hesitated at first; nobody had ever asked to see her grade book before. Yes, her principal had reviewed her lesson plans, but not her *grade book*. I found that she had various notations for students on activities across all of the subjects; some were numbers, some were in color, and some seemed like code. LeeAnn Morrill, a high school language arts teacher, showed me her grade book—an electronic display of individual student names and a vast number of activities categorized as homework, quizzes, tests, daily work, and projects; each activity had a percentage score attached to it.

When I asked Peggy and LeeAnn if their grade books documented the feedback they'd given students in order to improve benchmark-related knowledge, both answered in the same way: "The plan book is where you would find the benchmarks and objectives. The grade book is where you see the student grades on the activities that are tied to the benchmarks."

Breaking out of this paradigm is where we can begin to improve the feedback we give to students. In many cases, the teachers' plans *do* relate to benchmarks and objectives, but as the teachers deliver the lessons, they don't deliberately monitor student work and give feedback to students by benchmark criteria. Instead, each student receives feedback on the activity, whether it's a worksheet, quiz, test, project, paper, class participation, and so on. This feedback most often takes the form of points awarded for accuracy and task completion and only ambiguously addresses the benchmarks or objectives. Students know how many points they earned or lost on the assignments, but that feedback does not directly address their content understandings or procedural abilities. But because a relationship exists between the lessons and the grades, this form of feedback *seems* to work.

Consider the alternative to scoring by activities: scoring by benchmarks. In *Assessment, Grading, and Record Keeping* (Marzano, Zeno, & Pollock, 2000), my colleagues and I discuss scoring by academic or nonacademic criteria rather than scoring to activities organized under the categories of homework, class assignments, quizzes, tests, and so on. To do this, however, teachers must modify their grade books and their record-keeping practices.

Peggy and LeeAnn were both willing to make these modifications. They began by generating a list of concerns they had about scoring students by benchmarks:

- What do I do first?
- Do I still give grades?
- Do I use percentages or letter grades?

- Should I grade homework?
- Should I grade effort?
- How many grades do I need for each benchmark?
- What if a student misses an assignment?
- Do I have to use a rubric for every benchmark?
- Do I have to use an electronic grade book?
- Should I give the benchmarks to the students?
- Don't we have to change the report card now?

Although independently Peggy and LeeAnn both embraced a "keep it simple" approach, changing record keeping and grade books invariably complicates the conversation about student assessment and what to do about student performance. Thankfully, there are good resources available—such as Robert Marzano's *Transforming Grading* (2000) and Jim Popham's *The Truth About Testing* (2001)—that address the process and its attendant issues in a more technical manner than is possible here. Nonetheless, I do want to provide basic answers to questions Peggy and LeeAnn posed, as they are ones that many teachers have.

Questions About Revising Grading and Record-Keeping Practices

What do I do first?

Locate your curriculum benchmarks and students' names, and then set up your grade book. Whether you are using a computer program like Microsoft Excel or working in a paper grade book, you decide how you want to organize your grade book based on visual preferences and the nature of the subject area. Most teachers seem to have a clear preference for either a portrait orientation (students' names are displayed along the top of the document) or a landscape orientation (students' names are displayed along the left-hand side of the document). Some formatting examples include listing students vertically and sequential benchmarks horizontally (see Figure 5.1, p. 108) and vice versa (see Figure 5.2, p. 109). A variation calls for organizing by student rather than by benchmark: setting aside a separate page for each individual learner, then arranging the benchmarks either vertically or horizontally and filling in the opposite axis with tasks or dates of assignments (see Figures 5.3 and 5.4, pp. 110–111).

FIGURE 5.1

A Grade Book for Benchmark Scoring – Model 1

Student Names	Type the Benchmark Here						Type the Benchmark Here						Type the Benchmark Here						Type the Benchmark Here					
	Activity	Activity	Activity	Activity	Activity	Activity	Activity	Activity	Activity	Activity	Activity	Activity	Activity	Activity	Activity	Activity	Activity	Activity	Activity	Activity	Activity	Activity	Activity	Activity
Student 1																								
Student 2																								
Student 3																								
Student 4																								
Student 5																								
Student 6																								
Student 7																								
Student 8																								
Student 9																								
Student 10																								
Student 11																								
Student 12																								
Student 13																								
Student 14																								
Student 15																								
Student 16																								

FIGURE 5.2
A Grade Book for Benchmark Scoring – Model 2

Students	Student 1	Student 2	Student 3	Student 4	Student 5	Student 6	Student 7	Student 8	Student 9	Student 10	Student 11	Student 12	Student 13	Student 14	Student 15	Student 16	Student 17	Student 18	Student 19	Student 20	Student 21	Student 22
Type the benchmark here																						
Activity																						
Activity																						
Activity																						
Activity																						
Activity																						
Type the benchmark here																						
Activity																						
Activity																						
Activity																						
Activity																						
Activity																						
Type the benchmark here																						
Activity																						
Activity																						
Activity																						
Activity																						
Activity																						
Type the benchmark here																						
Activity																						
Activity																						
Activity																						
Activity																						
Activity																						

Benchmarks

FIGURE 5.3 A Grade Book for Benchmark Scoring – Model 3												
Student Names	E1.2.1 Know properties of Earth materials				E1.2.3 Understand differences in physical and chemical properties of Earth materials				E1.2.7 Know origin of fossils			
	Property #1	Property #2	Property #3	Unit Assessment	Difference #1	Difference #2	Difference #3	Unit Assessment	Origin #1	Origin #2	Origin #3	Unit Assessment

Source: Brenna Garrison-Bruden, Webster Stanley Elementary, Oshkosh, Wisconsin.

	FIGURE 5.4

A Grade Book for Benchmark Scoring – Model 4

Student Name: _____

Forces Benchmarks

Guiding/Topical Questions:
- What effect do forces have on various objects?
- How do we use forces to do work?
- How do simple machines help us do work?

Benchmark #	Benchmarks	Score
D3.2.1	Understand the effect of forces. * Describe what happens to an object when forces of various strengths are applied to it * Compare a variety of forces used to do the following: move objects, speed up, slow down, change the position of objects * Compare the effect of the same force on a variety of objects * Compare the effect of the same force on the same object on varied surfaces * Sort or classify objects according to how they respond to forces	_____ _____ _____ _____ _____
D3.2.2	Understand that objects in motion move in different ways. * Straight line * Zigzag * Curve * Vibration * Circular motion	 _____ _____ _____ _____ _____
D3.2.3	Know the properties of magnets. * Attract certain metals while not attracting others * Classify objects according to whether they attract magnets or not * Repel like poles * Natural and manufactured * Uses	 _____ _____ _____ _____ _____
D3.2.4	Understand simple machines. * Compare types of simple machines * Identify how simple machines are used * Explain why simple machines are used	 _____ _____ _____
G1.2.2	Understand that throughout history, people everywhere have invented and used technology. Today's technology is different from technology of the past. However, much of the technology today is a modification of very ancient tools.	_____
H1.2.1	Understand that there is no perfect design. Designs that are best in one respect may be inferior in other ways, and the solution to one problem may create other problems.	_____
Overall Unit Score		_____

Source: Jodie Jantz, Goodrich Middle School, Lincoln, Nebraska.

Each model has its advantages and disadvantages, but most important is the individual teacher's preference for organizing the data in a way that will make it easy to detect patterns of performance. Electronic grade book programs do not always offer multiple formatting options but may, in turn, offer a useful relational database. These allow the teacher to input benchmark scores for various tasks and, later, generate reports.

I recommend that teachers try this manual, "doing it by hand" exercise first, which helps clarify the logic behind assigning multiple scores to a task or to a benchmark. Once they understand the methodology, electronic scoring programs can increase efficiency and accuracy of the data.

"How do I organize the benchmarks for the year?" Peggy asked. At first she wanted to set up her electronic spreadsheet like the one depicted in Figure 5.1. Once she tried to use it, though, she changed her mind. Peggy recognized immediately that she wanted two different views of the benchmarks. A sequential system worked for language arts, but she wanted her benchmarks organized by unit for math, science, and social studies. Once she organized those subjects by unit, she realized that some benchmarks, such as those for inquiry and computation, appeared in more than one unit, so she decided she wanted to separate out those benchmarks.

Peggy also noted that in science, she would score to the benchmark, but the daily objective and activity were one and the same. Understanding this, she wrote scores for the daily objectives, a cluster of which tied to the benchmark. In those cases, the students received a daily objective score and a benchmark score. In her grade book, the objective activity scores were simply organized under a benchmark.

Secondary language arts teacher Pam Slawson found herself dealing with a related issue. When she organized her benchmarks by unit, she identified criteria she wanted to separate entirely from academic scoring. She decided to create a separate section in her grade book for tracking student homework, participation, and effort using an "Approach to Learning" scale. On a given assignment, she could write one score for the benchmark, then flip the pages in her grade book to write a score for the "approach to learning." Likewise, if a teacher wanted to use character education criteria, such as those suggested by

Sean Covey in *The Seven Habits of Highly Effective Teens* (1998), then the students and teacher could track these separately from the content benchmarks and objectives.

At first this approach sounds like more scoring and more grading, but the differences are significant. When teachers grade by activities, it's nearly impossible to unpack the resulting data to show where the student needs to make gains. However, when teachers score by deconstructing an activity score into different benchmarks in the grade book, patterns emerge and become useful for describing the learner's performance, giving specific feedback about it, and making decisions about what to do next.

Do I still give grades?

The generally accepted vernacular of grading (i.e., giving or receiving "a grade") implies the comprehensive or summative score on a report card or, to some, a test grade indicated by a letter (*A, B, C,* and so on) or percentage score. Yes, teachers using the Big Four will still give grades to each student for each subject area.

Scores in LeeAnn's previous grade book were represented by percentages for different activities, including quizzes or tests. At the end of the term, she averaged those scores, weighting certain assessments as more important. Today, she still evaluates student work but assigns scores by benchmarks. An assignment may address one or more benchmark statements; a test may also cover one or more benchmarks. After writing scores for various assignments (including observations), she "eyeballs" or analyzes the scores to note trends and patterns of performance. "That is the difference," she comments. "I still grade; it is just that I organize the scores in a different way [by benchmarks] so that I am more able to see the student learning trends in the content."

In some cases, she weights the test grades and the classroom assignments differently, because one indicates instruction-prompted performance and the other indicates independent assessment. At the end of the term, scores are consolidated (not averaged) by benchmarks; benchmark scores are consolidated by standards; and standard scores are consolidated for a final grade.

Do I use percentages or letter grades?

Teachers who score by benchmarks often realize that percentage or point scoring can be restrictive, so they begin to use a scale that mimics the college 4.0 scale or the state testing scales (e.g., advanced, proficient, basic, and minimal). They may even come to feel that percentages and points are unnecessary when scoring to the content statements. In *Wad-ja-get? The Grading Game in American Education* (1971), Kirschenbaum, Simon, and Napier explain how percentage scoring evolved; the historical perspective makes previous grading techniques seem antiquated now that we have robust academic and life-skill benchmarks available.

Many teachers already using scoring rubrics (e.g., four- or six-point scales) for classroom assessment tasks realize the efficiency of the rubric-like scale both for informing the learner and managing record keeping. The most common rubric-like scoring is a four-point scale that fits with many state testing scales:

> 4 = Advanced
> 3 = Proficient
> 2 = Basic or Partially Proficient
> 1 = Minimal
> 0 = Not enough information to evaluate, or not complete

When using the above scale, teachers look to the benchmark statement to provide a description of what constitutes a proficient performance. For example, a physical education benchmark might read as follows:

> Uses beginning strategies for net and lead-up games. A student must perform the following specific content objective skills consistently in order to receive a score of "3" or proficient:
> — Keeps object going with partner using striking pattern.
> — Places ball away from opponent in a racket sport.
> — Hand and foot dribbles while preventing an opponent from stealing.

A student who performs these skills with unusual grace, tactic, or creativity receives a "4." A student who can improve with practice or effort receives a "2" or "1," and a student who does not execute enough plays to generate a judgment receives a "0."

With benchmarks, teachers can use rubric-like scoring and a generic scale like the one described above. Just as is done in percentage or letter-grade scoring, the teacher must identify the cut-off score to indicate that the performer has met a level of proficiency. On a four-point scale, three is generally considered proficient, but again, that is an individual decision. Teachers who score by benchmarks using the four-point scale usually are required to accommodate a district-approved grading program for reporting purposes. Kristie Lyon and Janae Pritchett, secondary advanced math teachers in Crested Butte, Colorado, aligned a four-point system with both the percentage and letter-grade systems required by their district.

Camille Leisten, a 3rd grade teacher at Franklin Elementary School in Oshkosh, Wisconsin, wrote about the scale the teachers in her school had devised:

We are trying to develop a four-point scale for assessment that will be used throughout our school. We want to create a set of descriptors that are kid-friendly, because the children will be exposed to them from kindergarten through 5th grade. After consulting with the district office, we were told that the entire district will be using the terms "advanced," "proficient," "basic," and "minimal" in the future. I'm guessing these will be used on our new report card. We also wanted to continue to use "secure," "developing," and "beginning" in our classrooms (not on the report card) because we use them currently in our math program and the children are familiar with them. So, keeping that in mind, we came up with the following scale and descriptors:

Advanced (Secure +)
I have an advanced understanding of the learning goals and can use them by myself.

Proficient (Secure)
I need little or no help to understand and use the learning goals.

Basic (Developing)
I need some help to understand and use the learning goals.

Minimal (Beginning)
I need a lot of help to understand and use the learning goals.

You might ask, *Shouldn't the department, school, or district agree on grading?* Logically, yes, but until those decisions are made, an individual teacher can still begin to score by benchmarks using a rubric-like scale to provide better feedback and more meaningful data to the student. Aligning this scoring with district-mandated scoring may require converting scores to percentages or letter scores for reporting purposes.

Should I grade homework?

As you've read, Gary Nunnally admits to having been a gradeaholic. He's told me that he used to assign homework daily and insist that students earn a grade for it because, he reasoned, the grade would motivate them to do the work. Homework assignments were collected, graded, and returned, sometimes a few days later. Gary says that he believed that taking points off homework turned in late motivated students to get the homework done on time. (He had plenty of evidence that it didn't.) He created extra-credit assignments for students to offset the points taken off on homework. Eventually, he began to feel like he was playing croquet in Alice's Wonderland. What were the rules? What was he trying to accomplish? Why was he so focused on the behavioral aspect of homework?

Now recovered from his affliction, Gary offers a few rules of thumb to his students regarding homework:

> — Homework counts. You will receive a plus (+) or minus (–) or *I* (incomplete). A general homework score will be included and weighted in final grades.
> — Homework may be part of a longer assignment, so it may also be part of an academic grade.
> — Homework is part of your class notebook.
> — Homework might be reviewed at the beginning of a lesson for correction or might be used during a lesson as background notes or information.

— When you do homework consistently, you tend to do better on quizzes and tests.

Whether or not to assign homework is a controversial issue, but a teacher who assigns it should always comment on it verbally or in writing when the individual student needs feedback. Because homework is not supervised and not considered "high stakes," it can often be self- or peer-evaluated. You can still assign and write a score for it in the grade book, either for content (a rubric-like score) or completion (+ or –).

Many teachers assign homework for other reasons, such as teaching a student appropriate study behaviors. In these cases, they often find that a completion score gives the necessary task feedback, but that the content score is likely tied to work completed during class time. When it comes time to give a grade for the term, teachers use the benchmark scores for tests and quizzes to indicate proficiency, and homework scores often fall in the category of effort.

Should I grade effort?

Yes, both teachers and individual students should track effort scores. Similar to homework, effort can be assigned a plus (+) or minus (–) score and kept separately from the content scores in the same way that Pam Slawson kept the "approaches to learning" scores separate in her grade book from her language arts benchmarks. The experiences of middle school math teachers Vickie Barry and Katie Pease corroborate research indicating that effort can have a direct effect on the success a student has in math. Every day in Vickie's and Katie's classes, students complete an assignment sheet with a space to record the self-assessed effort score and task scores (see Figure 5.5, p. 118). Over time, the students discuss the patterns of how high or low scores on effort relate to the high or low scores in math. Both teachers describe the positive effect that this has had on the middle school students' math performances. It didn't happen immediately, they noted, but once the students got into the routine, the data began to work to show them how to improve performance.

FIGURE 5.5
A Student Effort and Understanding Self-Assessment

Math 8 Objectives

Chapter: _____

Name: _____   Period: _____

Overall personal goal for the chapter: _____

Plan for achieving this goal: _____

Date for achieving this goal: _____

Date	Text Section	Objective/Goal for the Day	Class Effort Rating (0–5)	HW Score	Understanding Rating (0–5)

Source: Vickie Barry and Katie Pease, Goodrich Middle School, Lincoln, Nebraska.

How many grades do I need for each benchmark?

A principal friend from Wyoming once told me that a rider in a bronco riding event needs to perform 10 rides on consecutive days in order to earn a cumulative score that is considered to be an accurate indicator of his performance. Assessment expert Grant Wiggins has answered the "how many grades" question many times by using the analogy that the diving judges at the Olympics need only three performances to discern an individual diver's pattern of performance and distinguish divers from one other. Assessing student performance in the classroom falls in between these two—around six scores is sufficient to establish the pattern of performance.

Here's an example. For a student to receive a legitimate grade on a family and consumer-studies benchmark such as "Understands that the stages of the family life cycle affect housing needs, including physical disabilities," the learner spends four or five class periods learning the specific content of mobility and ease of movement, location and climate, and public services or cultural offerings. During instruction, each activity allows the teacher to score the student on specific content objectives and, more generally, to the benchmark. The teacher records multiple scores and notes that these are tied to benchmarks, as shown in the activity spaces in Figures 5.1 through 5.3.

This concept is much more practical than it sounds. When a teacher considers observation as legitimate assessment, he or she can give feedback and record scores during instructional activities, such as discussions, in addition to using graded papers. Secondary teacher Jeff See explains his approach: "My goal is to know how well my students perform on the benchmark. For some students, I have to track more observation or informal scores than for others depending on how well they show their understandings, but I always track the quiz, test, essay, and project scores for all students."

What if a student misses an assignment?

When a teacher asks this question as it relates to scoring by benchmarks, I respond by asking a question of my own: "What happened if a student missed an assignment before you were scoring to benchmarks?" Many tell me that they would take off points, depending upon the excuse. Others say they'd accept assignments without taking off points up to a certain time. Even in a department or across a grade level, teachers do not seem to reach consensus on this issue.

Gary found that once he started giving students their grades and feedback by benchmark criteria, students were less likely to have truant assignments. And because the assignments had become more valuable to him (as evidence of performance), he was more interested in encouraging students to complete them instead of focusing, as he had, on taking off points as a means to manage student behavior.

Do I have to use a rubric for each benchmark?

No, a rubric is an assessment task tool with a very specific job of providing detailed feedback to a learner. It is rightly used when given in advance of the task. Historically, prolific use of rubrics in our classrooms coincided with the 1980s wave of authentic assessments. Once students performed on authentic tasks, teachers had to use a scoring methodology in order to track performance on whole projects. Finding percentage scoring inappropriate, teachers looked to rubrics because they displayed criteria and the expected performance details on a single page. We learned to use analytic scoring rubrics instead of holistic scoring rubrics so as to distinguish certain performance criteria from others and give better feedback.

Without question, students like rubrics because they guide performance expectations. Once standards and benchmarks were introduced, however, it was clear that the criteria on the rubric and the benchmark were one and the same. Today we find that when a student knows the benchmark, the benchmark itself often comprises enough information to allow us to score it with "rubric-like scoring" or provide a generic rubric.

When the teacher needs to give a student more explicit feedback (on writing assignments, for example), it is appropriate and necessary to use a rubric because of the breadth of detail assigned to each of the traits of writing. Many teachers find that if they create various generic rubrics based on benchmarks for presentations or working with others, they can be shared with other teachers at the same grade level.

Do I have to use an electronic grade book?

In some cases, districts have purchased student information systems that include a grade book component. If, however, that grade book follows a more traditional grading program format, teachers find it easier to use alternates, such as a stand-alone program, spreadsheets in Microsoft Excel, or even tables in Microsoft Word. In one case I'm familiar with, although the district required all teachers to use a specific program to generate report cards, teachers surveyed stated that they tracked data in various ways: in electronic grade books, in traditional paper grade books, and by using a spreadsheet.

More recently, however, programs have become available that allow benchmark scoring, benchmark reporting, and a summary version of those for a standards-based report card.

Should I give the benchmarks to the students?

Teachers, especially those in the upper grades, should consider giving their students the benchmarks, organized by the units of study. For example, middle school science teachers Jodie Jantz and Dan Shafer give the benchmarks to students at the beginning of each unit; this works as an advance organizer as well as a tool for the students to self-assess.

In primary grades, giving benchmarks to students in advance does not have the same practical value. Teachers in Wisconsin's Howard-Suamico School District, however, took the time to rewrite the benchmarks in "kid" language to use with students and parents in conferences and portfolios. Second grade teacher Brenna Garrison-Bruden, in Wisconsin's Oshkosh District, shows the benchmark spreadsheet to her students so they can track their own performances by benchmark across various assignments. She incorporates their self-assessment into her assessment and evaluation grades.

Don't we have to change our report cards now?

Although I hesitate to put it in print, when asked this question, I always respond with the following advice: Get off the Report Card Committee! What I mean is that until you have something different to report, don't change the report card; it has been functioning adequately up to now. Your pedagogical energy is much better spent in the classroom, working on your feedback strategies. When you start noticing changes, *then* think about changing the report card.

Another reason to hold off is that teachers who have become familiar with scoring by benchmarks can suggest better changes to the report card. Although the teacher's initial impulse may be to send "benchmark reports" home, parents, like students, have become accustomed to the grading-by-subject-area system characterized by letter grades or percentages. They are often more accepting of these reports when they are presented during conferences, where there is time to discuss the student's performance.

If, however, your district is committed to changing the report card, it is prudent to consider generating a report card that might include standards at the K–5 or K–8 levels, or maybe some selected standard-specific benchmarks (e.g., literacy or math) at the K–5 levels. I do not recommend changing the secondary transcript from course titles with grades because many colleges use those two criteria for decisions on admissions. In summary, you can work on the report card as a way of initiating the discussion about learning to score by benchmarks in grades K–12.

Verbal and Written Feedback

Every teacher already gives verbal and written feedback. Sixth grade teacher Emily Kowal notes, "Once I started to score students by the content and life-long learning benchmarks instead of by activities, I found myself changing the way I operated in the classroom. Soon my verbal and written interaction with the students changed because we both became more focused by the targets. My 'checking for understanding' was no longer characterized by task management questions or comments, but true cueing and questioning about levels of understanding or practicing."

Middle school art teacher Jeff Lee sent me this e-mail:

> I was finishing up my assessment of a jewelry project that my students worked on for a few days. Because of the project's difficulty, I'd spent a lot of time helping students one-on-one. And I hadn't taken the time at the beginning to prepare a scoring sheet.

The old me would have simply blown off the feedback and told students to come in after class if they were having trouble. Now I'm seeing how important it is for that feedback to be immediate and useful. And most kids wouldn't come in after class (which, regrettably, is probably why I would have suggested that in the past).

Now, looking at these pieces and trying to assess them, I'm realizing that I didn't give daily feedback to everyone. I also didn't write down any notes, so I'm not exactly sure who got help and who did not. Because I wasn't able to sit down with every student during the project, now I feel that they could be missing out. So I'll design an enrichment activity tomorrow while I talk with each student. But that's not something I want to continue doing. Now I understand what you meant by tracking the data.

Like Emily and Jeff, most teachers find that criterion-based feedback soon extends into both their verbal interactions and the written feedback they provide to students on daily assignments or projects.

External Measures

In this age of accountability, external measures or state tests sometimes seem to take priority over classroom assessment. How do we align the critically important practice of classroom assessment with the non-negotiable (for the time being) practice of external or state testing? Assessment researcher Don Burger suggested creating a simple grid he called a *calibration matrix*. The students with As in the class should receive "advanced" scores on the state test; those with Bs should receive "proficient" scores; and so on (personal correspondence, May 2006). If discrepancies arise, the teacher knows she has, at the very least, a grading problem.

In addition, Gayle Frame, former assistant superintendent of Howard-Suamico School District, writes that when the teachers in her district began to score by benchmarks, their state test scores improved:

In 1998, four years after the curriculum process began, three of the four elementary schools achieved unusually close scores in science, despite both socioeconomic differences between the schools and wide disparity in scores on other content areas of the test. For the next two years, 1999 and 2000, the science test scores between the highest and lowest scoring schools not only narrowed, but the percentage of students scoring in the proficient and advanced categories significantly increased.

In 1999 and 2000, the district also saw improvement in scores for mathematics, reading/language arts, and social studies. By 2000, test results for schools with the highest percentage of low socioeconomic students improved across all core content areas, and the test score gap narrowed between the highest- and lowest-scoring schools.

We believe that the initiative to train teachers to score students by robust learning targets (benchmarks) was responsible for the improvement gains in science, math, and English between 1998 and 2000 on the state assessments.

What worked? What seems obvious now, but was revolutionary at the beginning, is that identifying standards and grade-level benchmarks unified many of our organizational practices around the learner. In the past, school improvement goals and staff development targeted curriculum, instruction, and assessment, but they often operated in isolation; we also believed Herbart's old curriculum conviction that if you "improve the teacher," you automatically "improve the learner." Redefining curriculum with K–12 standards and benchmarks brought staff development efforts and school improvement goals (student learning) together for the first time.

The improvement model for this district was based on the Big Four, and the efforts of each individual teacher led to significant gains in student learning districtwide.

Teacher Voice

Jodie Jantz

Middle school science teachers are particularly fun to talk with when data and an experiment are involved, and Jodie is no exception. She approached reflecting on and adjusting her planning and scoring as a "lab." The results? Jodie found that the Big Four's complex integration of proven practices gave her the clarity she needed to improve learning in her classroom. As Jodie worked through the changes she made, she kept her eye on the prize—student learning—while negotiating what she needed to do as a teacher to make the changes manageable.

⋯⋯⋯

I HAVE BEEN A TEACHER OF SCIENCE FOR THE PAST 12 YEARS. I SAY A "TEACHER OF SCIENCE" and not a "science teacher" because I have always felt that my bag of tricks for teaching scientific concepts was very deep—like an army duffel—whereas my bag of tricks for teaching students was more like, well, an evening purse.

I did a great job with the student who came ready to learn, but I always struggled to reach those who weren't as well prepared. It wasn't that these students lacked IQ points or an interest in science, but the same hands-on learning and worksheets didn't seem to hook them and help them learn the concepts that I thought all students needed to learn. My problem magnified when my district started administering five districtwide criterion-referenced exams each year to all students at my grade level. As a teacher who had been on the committee that wrote the standards and curriculum documents, and who had also evaluated the test questions and piloted the tests, I felt that my students would do fine on just about any district exam.

Imagine my shock and concern when our first-year test results came back. Not only had my students not done as well as I expected, but their scores placed them in the bottom 2 of the district's 11 middle schools. Convinced that my students were just as good and smart as any student in our district, I redoubled my efforts! I incorporated more hands-on learning tasks, more worksheets, and more verbatim notes; after all, we teach the way we were taught and this, I thought, would be what my students needed to score better on the exams the next year.

Can you guess what happened to my students' exam results the following year? Yep, they were at rock bottom. These were good, smart kids who, for the most part, completed just about any assignment I gave them. Why was it that they could not show this on a simple, 40-question, multiple-choice exam? There was only one answer left: *It must be me.* Maybe I just wasn't cut out to be a teacher.

This is where I was when my school started to work with the Big Four approach. We began looking closely at the fourth and second tenets: feedback and instructional strategies. We focused particularly on giving specific feedback in a timely manner, setting daily objectives so that students can see what the day's lesson will be about, and having students summarize what they've learned at the end of a lesson. The idea was to change the feedback being given to the students to help them learn better. To change feedback, we needed criteria (benchmarks and objectives), and then the students needed to summarize their learning of the objectives. Easy enough. In fact, I had done all of these at one time or another, just never in a systematic or consistent manner. Honestly, when past principals had advised me to do these things, I thought they were just trying to brainstorm random ideas to help me teach better. The Big Four caught my attention because it espoused what I really wanted to do: *help students learn better.*

I started trying to be more deliberate with my lesson planning on a daily basis. I set daily objectives for the students, as identified in the Teaching Schema for Master Learners. In the past I would have written, "Science Goal for Today: Complete Lab." After being introduced to the Big Four, I realized that my goal did not address any specific objectives found in my district standards. When I started looking at my district standards, I realized that they were pretty good concepts, but some needed unpacking to the SB and SBSC levels.

The standard that corresponded to my lab read like this: "Investigate Newton's first and third Laws of Motion through experimentation." In order to set this as an objective and score to it, I unpacked it as follows:

Understand Newton's first and third laws and how they explain the motion of an object.
• Define Newton's first and third laws, as well as motion, inertia, force, acceleration, mass, speed, and velocity.
• Be able to calculate speed = distance/time, velocity = speed in a direction, and acceleration = final velocity − initial velocity/ time.
• Demonstrate the ability to collect and graph data.
• Demonstrate the change in motion of an object, and use Newton's first and third laws to explain the results.

I told the students that if they could complete the activities and applications for each of the specific content objectives, then they would understand why the motion of an object changes and be able to explain that motion using Newton's first and third laws. Using a variety of formative assessments, I evaluated each student individually on the specifics of the lesson, traced back to the benchmark. The students liked this approach because it seemed to them that they were getting multiple chances to understand the material and not just separate activities that added up to a grade in science.

This approach was better. Students came in, sat down, took out their daily starter sheet, and recorded the objective; I was surprised that they honestly seemed interested in finding out how we were going to meet the benchmarks. Formative and summative assessments quickly showed that all of my ready-to-learn students and a few of my strugglers were helped by this one change.

Energized, I started working on having students summarize their learning at the end of each lesson. This took many forms: journal entries, exit questions, group responses, verbal summarization, and sometimes a picture or pictograph. Again, the approach seemed to make my ready-to-learn students and a few more of my strugglers more task-oriented.

Then, it came time for our first district criterion-referenced test (CRT) of the year. I held my breath and nearly cried when the results came back: My students had increased their overall proficiency by 29 percentage points over the previous year's students. This placed them 5th in the district, instead of 10th out of 11 schools.

Elated at these results, I went back to creating a change in my classroom with a vengeance. If just setting the objectives and having students summarize back to them had caused this effect, imagine what would happen if I got serious about my feedback to the students? What if I didn't just say and write "good job" or "nice drawing" but instead took the time to write, "If your lab conclusion is _____ , what does that say about _____?"

Time = Lunch × Planning × After School

I suspect that you're thinking, "That's fine for you. You probably have 50 students and live alone with your seven cats! You have plenty of time to write wordy feedback." The truth is, I have about 120 students on average and live with three children and a spouse, and one of my strongest reservations about implementing these changes was related to all the paperwork I was creating for myself. I also continued to ponder the nagging question of how to grade all this work my students were doing. Should each daily sheet be worth 50 points? How about labs? Quizzes? The summarizing students were doing? If you examined my grade book, I looked super because the number of Ds and Fs in my classes had dropped dramatically, from about 20 percent to 10 percent. But it was possible this was only because of the sheer number of assignments I had given that quarter.

If my goal was to try to bring up my school's test score on one set of CRTs, I had proven that I could do it, but could I really keep up the pace? I was spending two hours a day grading and giving feedback. Was that really the goal I wanted for myself? Shouldn't my goal be to ensure that when my students leave, they understand all of the science standards we just spent the last 178 days working on?

The answer to this last question, of course, was a resounding yes, so back to the drawing board I went. I had done all of this work writing and adjusting objectives, helping students summarize, and giving better feedback. What did I need to do to ensure that all students were learning all of the science content and processes recommended by the standards? I'm embarrassed to admit this, but the "teacher of science" *finally* realized that the only answer was to collect some data. Apparently I have to "touch the stove" three times.

Using the Scientific Method Myself

I started simple. This meant giving a prequiz and, in my grade book, identifying the student answers with a "yes" or "no" for their understanding of each vocabulary word and concept. It was my start on scoring to benchmarks. Now I could look down the list and know which students—at least on this particular quiz—knew which words and what concepts. This information changed the way I wrote the next day's lessons and assigned homework. It also changed the pace at which some classes proceeded. I couldn't just say, "Today, all students will be doing lab X or worksheet Y." Now some of my students needed to spend more time working with certain concepts, while others could move on to different concepts. I was differentiating instruction, and I had the data to back up both the need for the differentiation and the results of doing so.

This new approach also changed the way I wrote assignments for students. If I was trying to track students' learning based on the standards or benchmarks, I couldn't just create a worksheet about Newton's first law or a lab about Newton's third law; I needed to look carefully at what I included and left out so that my students could get enough practice with new concepts and vocabulary. My goal was to be able to point to a chart showing what each student knew about the science—and it couldn't be just a list with quiz or test numbers.

One of the most surprising things about this process was how it changed the grades my students received at the beginning of a quarter. Many students and parents were horrified to see a grade report indicating a science grade of C+ when the student had never before received anything below an A. It took most of the quarter to get my students and their parents to understand that even though the prequiz grade was an F, the subsequent grades on quizzes, homework, labs, lab reports, and tests went up and up as the student learned more and more about the concept. In the end, everyone said that once they understood the change, they liked that the grade sheet no longer said, "quiz X," "worksheet Y," but rather "can define motion," "can create a graph from data," "can collect data on the change in inertia of an object," and so on. At the end, my grade curve still looked the same, but now I could look a *C* student in the eye and say, "If you want to bring your grade up, here are the concepts you need to learn." It was no longer a matter of just telling them to work harder or turn in more homework.

Again, I can imagine you thinking, "But isn't that still a lot of work?" The answer is yes, it is. After just one quarter, I knew I needed to change my process still more. Consistently, students' exam scores were going up with each CRT (27 and 28 percentage points higher on the next district exams than the previous two years' scores). My students were better behaved and more on task because they could see that each science class had a goal, and they could look at their grade sheet and see how their effort affected their grade. No longer did they just come to me and say, "I need to bring up my grade; can I do some extra credit?" They started to ask questions like "If I learn concepts *X* and *Y*, will my grade go up?" Still, the question remained: How to make less work for me?

The Law of (Self-) Reflection

During the last quarter of the year, I still give feedback, set objectives, help students summarize, and tie grades to the district standards, but instead of spending many hours collecting and compiling all the data, I have students begin to track some of their own data. When we start to look at each new concept, I give all students an assignment chart and a vocabulary/concept chart. Each day, as we work on different assignments, students write down the assignment and their effort. As I return papers to them, or as we grade things in class, they mark "yes" or "no" on their understanding of the concepts and vocabulary. I continue to track some data—prequizzes, formative questions, pop quizzes, and selected other work—but I don't do it every day. The payoff, aside from me not having so much to record, is evident in something that happened last week in class. We had been working with the law of reflection and had just completed one of my favorite labs. As we summarized the lesson's main point at the end of the period, one student noted that most people still couldn't tell me what the law of reflection meant, and another suggested we talk some more about it the next day instead of moving on to our next concept.

Could this be? Students taking responsibility for their own learning? I *can't wait* to see this quarter's test scores!

Afterword

Look at your fish.

—Louis Agassiz

IN HIS BOOK BRAVE COMPANIONS (1992), DAVID MCCULLOUGH DESCRIBES A UNIQUE professor at Harvard in the 1840s. McCullough recounts the story of how ichthyologist Louis Agassiz used unusual, but effective and memorable, teaching techniques with his doctoral students.

A student would enter the professor's office expecting an assignment or interview. Instead, Agassiz would show to the student to a seat in the laboratory and place in front of him a tray topped with a smelly, dead fish. "Look at your fish," Agassiz would advise the student, and then he would leave the room. An hour later, the professor would return, and the student, trying to please, would describe his observations. Agassiz would listen, then repeat, "Look at your fish. What do you see?"

Invariably, Agassiz's students counted scales, drew likenesses, measured, dissected, took notes, and comprehensively ascertained all there was to know about the fish. After repeating this scenario various times over a couple of days, Agassiz would ask the student, "Do you see the fish yet?" What he was doing was encouraging his students to *know something well*. The idea was that "discoveries are as likely to be found in material already in hand, before your eyes, as anywhere" (McCullough, 1992, p. xi).

I felt humbled by this story because it made me realize that to know about learning and improving student performance, we educators would do well to take Agassiz's advice and "look at our fish." The discoveries about learning we seek are likely waiting for us in the material already in our hands. What are "our fish" in the place called school?

Look at your plan book and your grade book. What can you know about your students' learning by looking deeply at your lesson plans and how they tie into the documented assessment or grades? Do the lessons you plan to deliver directly match the data that you track? What do your grades represent? Can they be dissected so that you can advise students how to improve in certain specific areas? Do the data show you how well students learned because you planned for it to happen in your classroom? Is there some purpose that connects the two "fish"—the plan book and the grade book?

Needs Assessment

Peggy Swick, coordinator for staff development for the Cooperative Educational Service Agency #6 (CESA 6) in Oshkosh, Wisconsin, observed that embracing the Big Four principles one teacher at a time works because it means each teacher takes responsibility for conducting a personal needs assessment with the goal of improving student learning. This, she notes, differs dramatically from other staff development offerings that tacitly promote district responsibility. Each teacher asks the following questions, assessing himself or herself on a five-point scale, with one being least compliant and five being most compliant.

1. *Do I have just-right learning targets?*   1   2   3   4   5

If not, what do I need to do to get them?

2. *Do I use a functional planning schema?*   1   2   3   4   5

If not, how do I adjust my planning to improve learning and not just to get me through the day?

3. *Do I vary assessment to elicit useful data?*   1   2   3   4   5

If not, what techniques do I need to incorporate into my classroom?

4. Does my feedback improve student performance?   1   2   3   4   5

If not, what verbal feedback and grading and record-keeping techniques will improve the feedback I give to students and, thus, improve their learning?

When high school teacher Mike Musil looked at his fish—conducted a personal needs assessment—he realized that his learning targets were not adequate, so he drafted a new set and started scoring by the benchmarks. After just one year, he reduced the numbers of *D*s and *F*s in his four classes from 30 to 3. Kent Swanson's fish revealed that years ago he had stopped requiring students to take notes in social studies because the students didn't do them very well; he reinstituted note taking for new information and began teaching strategies for taking notes. Once John Wright started scoring by his school's benchmarks, he found he had to face his hesitation about varying assessment, a common reluctance in math teachers. Jodie Jantz needed a schema, Vickie Barry sought to improve her verbal feedback to learners, and Michelle Crisatulli realized she needed to add thinking to the skills her 1st graders were learning. The 2nd grade teachers at Traeger Elementary School in Oshkosh, Wisconsin, changed their report cards because the old ones didn't clearly articulate the information they tracked about student learning.

When Gary Nunnally looked at his fish, he admitted that the feedback he gave to students, wrote in his grade book, and shared with parents was not helping students learn social studies—or study skills, for that matter. After a few significant pedagogical changes, he detected a change in students' learning; he then looked more deeply at his fish. His homework policy had been a way to mask instructional problems. His plan book, he admitted, was not designed for student learning but for covering chapters. His tests, he alleged, required recall, not application. So, he changed.

These teachers and so many others are our "brave companions." They are the teachers who look at their proverbial fish—the plan books and the grade books—and realize that history and research clearly show us that for students to improve, we need to improve our pedagogical practices . . . one teacher at a time.

Acknowledgments

My thanks to the following educators:

Michael Adams, Colegio Nueva Granada, Bogota, Colombia; Barbara Aiken, Columbus School, Medellin, Colombia; Maria Bagby, Colorado Department of Education, Denver, Colorado; Vickie Barry, Goodrich Middle School, Lincoln, Nebraska; Jeremy Cartier, Durgee Junior High School, Baldwinsville, New York; Conway Chewning, American International School of Budapest, Budapest, Hungary; Diane Clement, Escola Americana de Rio de Janeiro, Rio de Janeiro, Brazil; Michelle Crisafulli, Reynolds Elementary School, Baldwinsville, New York; Phil Eickstaedt, Oshkosh Area School District, Oshkosh, Wisconsin; Gayle Frame, Howard-Suamico School District, Green Bay, Wisconsin; Brenna Garrison-Bruden, Webster Stanley Elementary School, Oshkosh, Wisconsin; John E. Gates, Escola Americana de Brasilia, Brasilia, Brazil; Meegan Healey, Gunnison Middle School, Gunnison, Colorado; Jodie Jantz, Goodrich Middle School, Lincoln, Nebraska; Susan Jaramillo, Columbus School, Medellin, Colombia; John Koncki, Singapore American School, Singapore; Emily Kowal, Gunnison Middle School, Gunnison, Colorado; Linda Law, Baldwinsville School District, Baldwinsville, New York; Jeff Lee, Carey Junior High School, Cheyenne, Wyoming; Camille Leisten, Franklin Elementary School, Oshkosh, Wisconsin; Mike Loria, Columbus School, Medellin, Colombia; Kristie Lyon, Crested Butte Community School, Crested Butte, Colorado; Peggy Mihelich, Gunnison Community School, Gunnison, Colorado; LeeAnn Morrill, North High School, Oshkosh, Wisconsin; Jim Morris, Association of American Schools of South America; Mike Musil, North Star High School, Lincoln, Nebraska; Shelly Muza, Oshkosh Area School, Oshkosh, Wisconsin; Danny Neville, Cairo American College, Cairo, Egypt; Gary Nunnally, Waverly High School, Lincoln, Nebraska; Layne Parmenter, Urie Elementary School, Lyman, Wyoming; Marc Parrillo, Syracuse City School District, Syracuse, New York; Katie Pease, Goodrich Middle School, Lincoln, Nebraska; Dawn Preston, Baldwinsville School District, Baldwinsville, New York; Janae Pritchett, Crested Butte Community School, Crested Butte, Colorado; Diane Quirk, Baldwinsville School District, Baldwinsville, New York; Adriana Rocha, Columbus School, Medellin, Colombia; Stephen Rule, American School of Quito, Quito, Ecuador; Mary Virginia Sanchez, Association of American Schools of Central America; Jeff See, West High School, Oshkosh, Wisconsin; Dan Shafer, Goodrich Middle School, Lincoln, Nebraska; Pam Slawson, American International School, Dhaka, Bangladesh; Kent Swanson, Goodrich Middle School, Lincoln, Nebraska; Peggy Swick, Cooperative Education Service Agency #6, Oshkosh, Wisconsin; the staff of Traeger Elementary School, Oshkosh, Wisconsin; Ann Trovillion-Timm, Lincoln Public Schools, Lincoln, Nebraska; Corina Van Den Wildenberg, Dar Salaam School, Tanzania; and John Wright, Casablanca American School, Casablanca, Morocco.

In addition, my sincere thanks to the ASCD staff, in particular, my editor, Katie Martin.

References and Resources

Berliner, D. C. (1986). In pursuit of the expert pedagogue. *Educational Researcher* (August/September), 5–13.

Bernhadt, V. L. (1998). *Data analysis for comprehensive schoolwide improvement.* New York: Eye on Education.

Bloom, B. (Ed.). (1956). *Taxonomy of educational objectives.* New York: David McKay Company, Inc.

Coleman, J. S. (1966). Equality of Educational Opportunity Study (EEOS) [Computer file]. 2nd ICPSR version. Washington, DC: U.S. Department of Health, Education, and Welfare.

Cooney, W., Cross, C., & Trunk, B. (1993). *From Plato to Piaget.* Lanham, MD: University Press of America.

Costa, A. (Ed.). (1991). *Developing minds: A resource book for teaching thinking.* Alexandria, VA: Association for Supervision and Curriculum Development.

Costa, A., & Kallick, B. (2000). *Habits of mind: A developmental series.* Alexandria, VA: Association for Supervision and Curriculum Development.

Covey, S. (1998). *The seven habits of highly effective teens.* New York: Fireside.

Cremin, L. A. (1957). *The republic and the school: Horace Mann on the education of free men.* New York: Bureau of Publications, Teachers College, Columbia University.

Danielson, C. (2001, February). New trends in teacher evaluation. *Educational Leadership, 58*(5), 12–15.

Eggen, P. D., & Kauchak, D. P. (1988). *Strategies for teachers.* Upper Saddle River, NJ: Prentice-Hall.

Gagne, R. M. (1965). *The conditions of learning.* New York: Holt, Rinehart and Winston.

Glass, G. V., & Hopkins, K. D. (1984). *Statistical methods in education and psychology.* Upper Saddle River, NJ: Prentice-Hall.

Goodlad, J. I. (1984). *A place called school.* New York: McGraw-Hill.

Governor's Council on Model Academic Standards. (1998). *Wisconsin's model academic standards.* Madison, WI: Department of Public Instruction.

Gronlund, N. E. (1978). *Stating objectives for classroom instruction* (2nd ed.). New York: Macmillan.

Gutek, G. L. (1991). *Education in the United States: An historical perspective.* Boston: Allyn and Bacon.

Heiman, M., & Slomianko, J. (Eds.). (1987). *Thinking skills instruction: Concepts and techniques.* Washington, DC: National Education Association.

Hunter, M. (1982). *Mastery teaching.* Thousand Oaks, CA: Corwin Press.

Hunter, M. (1994). *Enhancing teaching.* New York: Macmillan College Publishing.

Hunter, R. (2004). *Madeline Hunter's mastery teaching.* Thousand Oaks, CA: Corwin Press.

Johnson, M. H. (1997). *Developmental cognitive neuroscience: An introduction.* Cambridge, MA: Blackwell Publishers.

Kendall, J. S., & Marzano, R. J. (1997). *Content knowledge: A compendium of standards and benchmarks for K–12 education.* Alexandria, VA: Association for Supervision and Curriculum Development.

Kirschenbaum, H., Simon, S. B., & Napier, R. W. (1971). *Wad-ja-get? The grading game in American education.* New York: Hart Publishing.

Mager, R. (1962). *Preparing objectives for programmed instruction.* Atlanta, GA: CEP Press.

Marzano, R. J. (2000). *Transforming grading.* Alexandria, VA: Association for Supervision and Curriculum Development.

Marzano, R. J., & Kendall, J. S. (1996). *A comprehensive guide to designing standards-based districts, schools, and classrooms.* Alexandria, VA: Association for Supervision and Curriculum Development.

Marzano, R. J., Pickering, D. J., Arredondo, D. E., Blackburn, G. J., Brandt, R. S., Moffett, C. S., & Pollock, J. E. (1992). *Dimensions of learning.* Alexandria, VA: Association for Supervision and Curriculum Development.

Marzano, R. J., Pickering, D. J., & Pollock, J. E. (2001). *Classroom instruction that works.* Alexandria, VA: Association for Supervision and Curriculum Development.

Marzano, R. J., Zeno, B., & Pollock, J. E. (2000). *Research into practice series: Assessment, grading, and record keeping.* Aurora, CO: McREL.

McCullough, D. (1992). *Brave companions.* New York: Simon and Schuster Paperbacks.

Ornstein, A., & Levine, D. (1987). *Foundations of education* (5th ed.). Boston: Houghton Mifflin.

Phillips, J. (1781). *The original deed of gift from John Phillips to Phillips Exeter Academy.* Available: http://library.exeter.edu/dept/Archives/deed.html

Popham, W. J. (2001). *The truth about testing: An educator's call to action.* Alexandria, VA: Association for Supervision and Curriculum Development.

Rosenshine, B. (1997). Advances in research on instruction. In J. W. Lloyd, E. J. Kameanui, & D. Chard (Eds.), *Issues in educating students with disabilities* (pp. 197–221). Mahwah, NJ: Lawrence Erlbaum. Available: http://epaa.asu.edu/barak/barak.html

Sadker, M. P., & Sadker, D. M. (1982). *Sex equity handbook for schools.* New York: Longman, Inc.

Snyder, T. (1993). *120 years of American education: A statistical portrait.* Available: http://nces.ed.gov/pubs93/93442.pdf

Sparks, D. (1998, Fall). Making assessment part of teacher learning: An interview with Bruce Joyce. *Journal of Staff Development, 19*(4). Available: http://www.nsdc.org/library/publications/jsd/joyce194.cfm

Stiggins, R. J. (1997). *Student-centered classroom assessment.* Upper Saddle River, NJ: Prentice Hall.

Stigler, J. W., & Hiebert, J. (1999). *The teaching gap.* New York: The Free Press.

Stigler, J. W., & Stevenson, H. W. (1992). *The learning gap.* New York: Summit Books.

Trumbull, E., & Farr, B. (2000). *Grading and reporting student progress in an age of standards.* Norwood, MA: Christopher-Gordon Publishers, Inc.

Tyler, R. (1949). *Basic principles of curriculum and instruction.* Chicago: University of Chicago Press.

U.S. Department of Education National Committee on Excellence in Education. (1983). *A nation at risk: The imperative for educational reform.* Washington, DC: Author. Available: www.ed.gov/pubs/NatAtRisk/index.html

U.S. Department of Labor Secretary's Commission on Achieving Necessary Skills. (1991, June). *What work requires of schools: A SCANS report for America.* Washington, DC: Author. Available: http://wdr.doleta.gov/SCANS/whatwork/whatwork.pdf

Wiggins, G. (1993). *Assessing student performance.* San Francisco: Jossey-Bass.

Online Resources

American Education Reaches Out: www.nesacenter.org/AERO

The Big 6: An Information Problem-Solving Process: www.big6.com

Developing Educational Standards: http://edstandards.org/Standards.html#Subject

Habits of Mind: www.habits-of-mind.net

Mid-continent Research for Education and Learning (McREL): www.mcrel.org

National Center for Education Statistics Publications Search Page: http://nces.ed.gov/pubsearch

National Council for the Social Studies: www.socialstudies.org

National Council of Teachers of Mathematics: http://nctm.org

No Child Left Behind: www.ed.gov/nclb/landing.jhtml

Northwest Regional Educational Laboratory's 6 + 1 Trait Writing for Assessment: www.nwrel.org/assessment/department.php?d=1

Index

Figures are indicated with an *f* following the page number.

About the Author

Jane E. Pollock works in the areas of assessment, grading and record keeping, curriculum and instruction, and supervision. Her previous school and district positions include classroom teacher, district K–12 curriculum coordinator, and state department staff development coordinator. She is the director of Learning Horizon, Inc., and an adjunct faculty member for the Association of Supervision and Curriculum Development, Buffalo State College, State University of New York, Viterbo College, Alverno College, and the International Teacher Training Center in Miami and London.

A native of Caracas, Venezuela, Dr. Pollock earned a bachelor's degree from Duke University and master's and doctorate degrees from the University of Colorado at Boulder. She conducts workshops and long-term curriculum projects worldwide, working with faculty to customize school curriculum based on national and international research aligned with assessments. In addition, she works side by side with teachers to develop curriculum guides, classroom lessons, assessments, and better record-keeping and reporting methods. With administrators, Dr. Pollock supports efforts to focus long-range planning and day-to-day classroom observations on giving teachers robust pedagogical feedback. The result of the work is increased student achievement, better communication among teachers, and better teaching practices.

Dr. Pollock is a coauthor of *Dimensions of Learning* and the *Dimensions of Learning Trainer's Manual;* two titles in the Research into Practice series (*Assessment, Grading, and Record Keeping* and *Effective Classroom Instruction*); and *Classroom Instruction That Works*. She can be reached by e-mail at learninghorizon@ msn.com.

Related ASCD Products: Teaching

For the most up-to-date information about ASCD resources, go to www.ascd.org. ASCD stock numbers are noted in parentheses.

Audio

The Best of the 2006 Teaching & Learning Conference - What Works in Schools: The Art and Science of Teaching (CDs: # 506204)

Mixed Media

Making School Improvement Happen with What Works in Schools: Teacher-Level Factors: An ASCD Action Tool by John L. Brown (#705054)

Teaching for Understanding: An ASCD Professional Inquiry Kit by Charlotte Danielson (#196212)

Online Professional Development

Go to ASCD's Home Page (http://www.ascd.org) and click on Professional Development to find ASCD's PD Online courses *Improving Student Achievement with Dimensions of Learning* and *The Reflective Educator*.

Print Products

Classroom Instruction That Works: Research-Based Strategies for Increasing Student Achievement by Robert J. Marzano, Debra J. Pickering, and Jane E. Pollock (#101010)

Enhancing Professional Practice: A Framework for Teaching (2nd edition) by Charlotte Danielson (#106034)

Habits of Mind: A Developmental Series edited by Arthur L. Costa and Bena Kallick (#100036)

A Handbook for Classroom Instruction That Works by Robert J. Marzano, Jennifer S. Norford, Diane E. Paynter, Debra J. Pickering, and Barbara B. Gaddy (#101041)

Qualities of Effective Teachers (2nd edition) by James H. Stronge (#105156)

Video

The How To Collection: Instruction That Promotes Learning (six 15-minute video programs on one 110-minute DVD) (#606141)

A Visit to Classrooms of Effective Teachers (one 45-minute program with a comprehensive Viewer's Guide) (DVD: #605026, videotape: #405026)

For more information, visit us on the World Wide Web (http://www.ascd.org), send an e-mail message to member@ascd.org, call the ASCD Service Center (1-800-933-ASCD or 703-578-9600, then press 2), send a fax to 703-575-5400, or write to Information Services, ASCD, 1703 N. Beauregard St., Alexandria, VA 22311-1714 USA.